9/03

The IQ Workout Series

INCREASE YOUR BRAINPOWER

Improve your creativity, memory, mental agility
and intelligence

Philip Carter and Ken Russell

JOHN WILEY & SONS, LTD
Chichester · New York · Weinheim · Brisbane · Singapore · Toronto

Published 2001 by John Wiley & Sons Ltd,
Baffins Lane, Chichester,
West Sussex PO19 1UD, England

National   01243 779777
International (+44) 1243 779777
e-mail (for orders and customer service enquiries):
cs-books@wiley.co.uk
Visit our Home Page on http://www.wiley.co.uk
or http://www.wiley.com

Other Wiley Editorial Offices

John Wiley & Sons, Inc., 605 Third Avenue,
New York, NY 10158-0012, USA

WILEY-VCH Verlag GmbH, Pappelallee 3,
D-69469 Weinheim, Germany

John Wiley & Sons Australia Ltd, 33 Park Road, Milton,
Queensland 4064, Australia

John Wiley & Sons (Asia) Pte Ltd, 2 Clementi Loop #02-01,
Jin Xing Distripark, Singapore 129809

John Wiley & Sons (Canada) Ltd, 22 Worcester Road,
Rexdale, Ontario M9W 1L1, Canada

British Library Cataloguing in Publication Data

A catalogue record for this book is available from the British Library

ISBN 0-471-53123-5

Typeset in 11/14 pt Garamond Book by Dorwyn Ltd, Rowlands Castle, Hants.
Printed and bound in Great Britain by Biddles Ltd, Guildford and King's Lynn.

This book is printed on acid-free paper responsibly manufactured from sustainable
forestry, in which at least two trees are planted for each one used for paper
production.

Contents

Introduction

The brain is the most vital organ in the human body and our most valuable asset. It gives rise to our perceptions and memory, and it shapes our speech, skills, thoughts and feelings, yet it is perhaps the part of our body which we tend to neglect the most.

This intricate web of nerves, which is the natural product of hundreds of years of evolution, somehow manages to regulate all the systems in the body, and at the same time absorbs and learns from a continual intake of new experiences.

Many of us take our brain for granted, believing there is little we can do to improve the brain we have been born with. This book sets out to demonstrate that this is not the case and that it is possible to considerably increase your brainpower and go some way to utilising your brain to its full potential.

Gymnasts are able to improve their performance, and increase their chances of success, at whatever level they are competing by means of punishing training schedules and refinement of technique. In the same way, we provide you with a series of mental gymnastics to give you the opportunity to maximise your brain potential.

This book is not intended as a text book about the structure and workings of the brain, although it is helpful to have some understanding about the composition of the brain itself, and this is provided briefly in the next section, 'About the brain'. The rest of the book concentrates on several main areas of brain function, namely creative thinking, memory, logical thought, agility of mind and intelligence, by means of a series of tests and exercises which are designed to be a fun way of stimulating brain activity in these areas.

We all have the capacity to put our brain to even more use by exploring new avenues, experiences and learning adventures. We believe this book will be just the start of such an adventure for many of our readers.

About the Brain

In vertebrates the brain is the portion of the central nervous system within the skull. In humans it is a mass of pink-grey tissue composed of about 100 billion nerve cells and weighing 3 lb (1.3 kg). Each of these brain cells is linked to another, and collectively they are responsible for the control of all mental functions.

The brain comprises less than 2% of total body weight but requires 25% of our oxygen intake and 70% of our glucose supply. The brain is not fully formed at birth, nor need it degenerate with age, as brain cells are constantly renewed and circuitry carrying its messages can be improved.

The brain is the control centre for virtually every vital activity necessary for survival including movement, sleep, hunger and thirst. In addition, all human emotions including love, hate, anger, elation and sadness, are controlled by the brain. It also receives and processes signals that are sent to it from other parts of the body and from sources external to the body.

The brain comprises three distinct but connected parts; the cerebrum, the cerebellum and the brain stem.

The largest part of the human brain is the cerebrum, which makes up approximately 85% of the brain's weight. It is an intricately developed part of the brain which accounts for the superior intelligence of humans, compared with other creatures. Its large surface area is called the cortex and

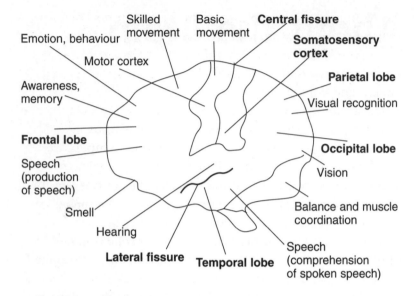

its complete functions are illustrated above. The cerebrum is
divided by a fissure into identical right and left hemispheres.

In turn each cerebral hemisphere is divided by fissures
into five lobes. Four of these lobes are named from bones of
the cranium; the frontal, parietal, temporal and occipital
lobes. The fifth lobe, the insula, is located internally and is
not visible at the outside of the brain.

The cerebellum lies in the back part of the cranium
beneath the cerebral hemispheres and is composed of two
hemispheres connected by white fibres called the vermis.
Three other bands of fibres (the cerebellar peduncles)
connect the cerebellum to other parts of the brain.

The cerebellum is essential to the control of movement of
the human body in space and acts as a reflex centre for
coordination and maintenance of equilibrium. It is this part
of the brain which controls all activity, from manipulating a
pair of knitting needles to a batsman smashing a ball to the
boundary.

The brain stem is made up of all the structures lying between the cerebrum and the spinal cord, and is divided into several components including the thalamus, hypothalamus, midbrain, medulla oblongata, pons, limbic system and cranial nerves.

These components regulate or are involved in many vital activities necessary for survival. The hypothalamus, for example, is concerned with eating, drinking, temperature regulation, sleep, emotional behaviour and sexual activity, and within the medulla are the vital control centres for cardiac and respiratory functions as well as other reflex activities, including vomiting.

Oxygen and glucose are supplied to the brain by two sets of cranial arteries known as the vascular system. Below the neck, each of the common carotid arteries divides into an external branch to supply the forward portion of the brain. The rest of the brain is supplied by the two vertebral arteries and these join together with the two internal carotid arteries to form the circle of Willis at the base of the brain. Of all the blood pumped by the heart, 25% is circulated within the brain tissue by a large network of cerebral and cerebellar arteries.

As can be seen in the above illustration, the cerebral cortex is subdivided into different functional areas.

The somatosensory area, located behind the central fissure, receives impulses from the skin surface as well as from beneath the skin and, therefore, possesses sensations such as touch and taste. In front of the central fissure is the somatomotor area which is responsible for voluntary movement of body muscles.

The area of the cortex concerned with hearing is the auditory area, which is in the upper part of the temporal lobe. The area for seeing, the visual cortex, is in the back portion, or occipital lobe, and the area governing our sense of smell, the olfactory area, is in the front portion of the temporal lobe. The area for language and speech, known as Broca's area, is responsible for the muscle movements of the throat and mouth used in speaking. Distinct from this is the area responsible for our understanding of speech and reading, which is between the auditory and visual areas.

A large portion of the cortex in humans is used for awareness, intelligence and memory. In this frontal area the memory of a new experience is stored within nerve cells in the brain. When seen again, the memory recalls and recognises this experience. We will discuss memory in greater detail later.

The human brain is an infinitely complex subject and these complexities are the subject of much debate. As technological methods become more advanced these issues will become increasingly clarified, as will treatments for abnormal diseases of the brain such as strokes, brain disorders, Parkinson's disease and cerebral palsy.

In the meantime we invite you to flex your mental muscles and indulge in mental activity to ward off neurodegeneration and make more and stronger connections between your nerve cells, with the result that not only your mental but also your physical well-being will improve.

Creativity

The term *creativity* refers to mental processes that lead to solutions, ideas, conceptualisation, artistic forms, theories or products that are unique and novel.

With many of us, much creative talent remains untapped throughout life. Until we try, we never know what we can actually achieve. We all have a creative side to our brain and, therefore, we all have the potential to be creative. Of course, some people are born to compose music, paint or have creative sporting talents; the young Mozart was composing music, for example, when he was four years old. On the other hand Anna Mary Robertson (1860–1961), better known as Grandma Moses, was a self-taught American artist who was for most of her life a farmer's wife. It was not until she was in her late 70s that she began to paint rural scenes for her own pleasure, and by the time she was 80 the Gallerie Saint Etienne in New York City presented her first solo exhibition, which launched her on a new career as an artist. The old adage 'you never know what you can do until you try' was never more appropriate than in this case.

Educationalists have a duty to encourage creative talents in all young people. However, this is not always the case. In today's world of specialisation many of these early talents are stifled and energies are channelled into one specific career, with the result that many latent talents remain undeveloped. By cultivating new leisure activities and pursuing new pastimes it is possible for each of us to exploit the potential, and often vastly underused parts, of the human brain.

Most of us have sufficient ammunition to realise this potential in the form of data which has already been fed into, collated and processed by the brain over many years. In music, for example, improvisation is the art of creating all or part of a composition at the moment of performance. To improvise efficiently a musician must understand the conventions of a given musical style. Such conventions provide a mental library for effective chord sequences and melody, which are used as a starting point for the improvisation. Such resources give the music cohesion while allowing room for spontaneous creativity.

The following exercises, while different in themselves, are all designed with the object of improving or recognising your own powers of mental productivity, generation of ideas and artistic skill.

Tests of creativity

1   In each of the following, study the line of figures and decide what pattern or movement is occurring, then draw what you consider to be the next figure in the sequence.

You have 30 minutes in which to complete the ten questions.

For example:

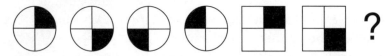

Answer:

Explanation: a set of circles, followed by a set of squares where the black quarter moves one place clockwise at each stage.

(i)

(ii)

(iii)

(iv)

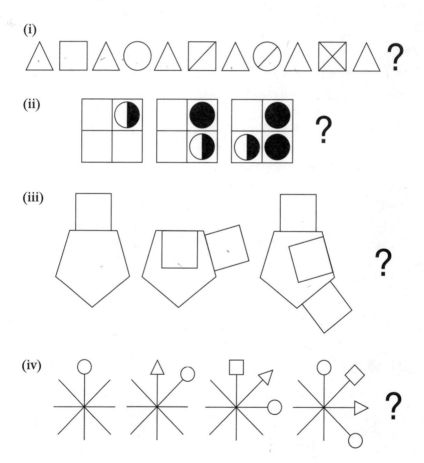

(v)

(vi)

(vii)

(viii)

(ix)

(x)

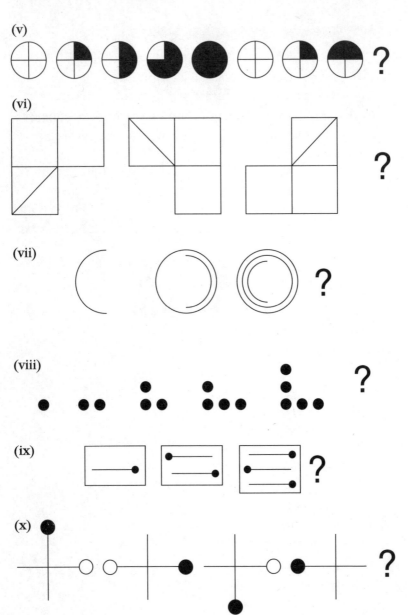

2   This puzzle will test your imagination and powers of lateral thinking.

Using matchsticks or cocktail sticks to build the pens and coins to represent the pigs, distribute nine pigs in four pens so that there will be an odd number of pigs in each pen.

3   This exercise will also test your creative imagination. It is based on the game of situation puzzles in which a mysterious situation is presented to a group of players, who must then try to find out what is going on by asking further questions. The person who initially presented the situation can only answer 'yes' or 'no', or occasionally 'irrelevant'.

In each of the following a certain mysterious situation is presented. It is up to you to use your imagination to find an explanation for how this situation could have occurred.

In the answers section we will give one such explanation. However, the more possible feasible explanations you can give the better.

(i)   A man is sitting in a restaurant in London reading a newspaper which he has just bought hot off the press. In the late news he reads 'Passenger lost overboard on Caribbean cruise'. He immediately realises a murder has been committed.

(ii) A man lies dead next to a cactus to which is stuck a piece of paper.

(iii) A man is driving a car alone down the road when the car suddenly swerves and crashes into a lamppost. People running to the scene immediately find the man slumped dead over the steering wheel with the bolt from a crossbow embedded in his back.

(iv) A man is lying in bed in his hotel bedroom unable to get to sleep. He makes one telephone call, says nothing, puts down the telephone and goes to sleep.

(v) A man is walking down the road when a stone gets stuck between his foot and his open-toed sandal. He leans against a pole, with his head down and shakes his foot to dislodge the stone. Another man rushes up and breaks his arm.

4   A rebus is the enigmatic representation in visual form of the sounds of a name or word. Rebus is a Latin word meaning *by things*, indicating a coded text which can be deciphered by studying its visual display.

Four examples are shown below which illustrate the type of creative thinking necessary to solve such riddles.

1	2	3	4
THE & EEEEE	**A·**	MEASU	TOCCDUN

1   The Andes (The and Es)

2   In a spot (a spot inside the letter A)

3   Short measures (the word measure is short of completion)

4   Disorderly conduct (TOCCDUN is an anagram of CONDUCT, its letters, therefore, presented in a disorderly fashion)

Now try the following, each one representing a familiar phrase.

There is no time limit; we are simply aiming here to put your powers of creative thinking to the test. For any that you cannot solve we suggest you return to them at a later time and have a fresh look. It is quite possible that the answer will suddenly come to you, as a result of your subconscious mind continuing to analyse the problem.

1	2	3
prERogative	T A R G E T	D L E A

4
N   N
  E   E
   V
  E   E
R   R
	5	6
		ITALY

7
     R
A
      I
  B
   N
	8
	POCILY
		9
		   P
		A S
		S I O N

10 AS TAT EOF	11 PATELLA LAMP	12 TUASPRF

5   The object here is to interpret each of the twenty drawings in the wildest and most imaginative way you

can. You may also try playing the game with other people. The more wild you think someone's suggestion, the better it is and the more creative they are. For example, you might think that drawing number 1 is the side of a tiled roof. But is there anything else it could be? Let your imagination run riot and see what you can come up with.

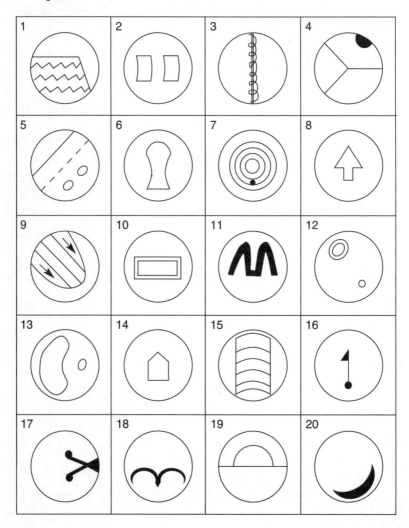

6 This test is based on Gestalt and Jackson's Test of
Divergent Ability, which requires the subject to name as
many new uses as possible for everyday objects such as a
brick or a piece of string.

Here, you are required to name up to 12 new uses for a
comb in 10 minutes.

You should work strictly to the time limit otherwise your
score will be invalidated.

1 ....

2 ....

3 ....

4 ....

5 ....

6 ....

7 ....

8 ....

9 ....

10 ....

11 ....

12 ....

7   We observe symmetrical patterns every day of our lives as they occur in nature and in designs such as wallpaper or tiling.

In this experiment we have created a symmetrical pattern in an array of hexagons. Following the ground rules already established, can you fill in all the remaining blank sections with the correct symbols to recreate the same symmetrical pattern?

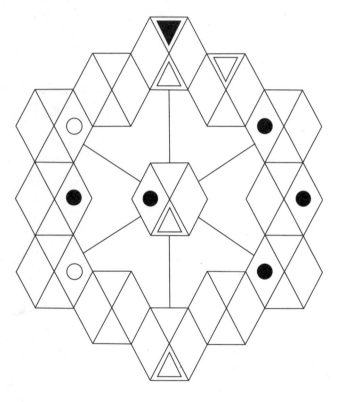

8 In each of the following use your imagination to create
   an original sketch or drawing of something recognisable
   incorporating the symbol already provided.

   You have 20 minutes in which to complete the six
   drawings.

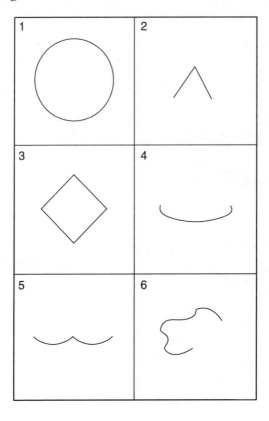

9 A man has an area of land containing 11 trees (T). He also has 22 cows and wishes to divide the land into 11 enclosures so that into each of these enclosures he can put two cows, which will then have just one tree for shelter. How can he divide up the land using as few fences as possible so that each enclosure contains just one tree?

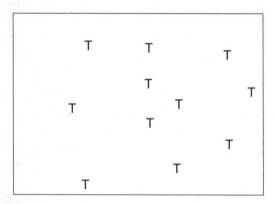

10 Make four cuts only of equal length to dissect the figure below into nine pieces that can be arranged to form four perfect squares all of the same size.

This is a difficult test and a hint is, therefore, provided on page 102.

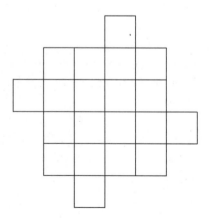

11 This presentation of a famous paradox is designed to stimulate creative thought and philosophical discussion.

For the sake of argument, I am retiring next week and am to be presented with a gift. However, the day of presentation is meant to be a surprise. In other words, although I know I am to receive the gift I do not know whether it is to be presented on the Monday, Tuesday, Wednesday, Thursday or Friday.

The question to consider is, can such a surprise gift ever be given? I know that it cannot be given on a Friday, the last day: for if it was left until then, the only day left, it would not be a surprise. So it must be on a Thursday. But then Thursday has in effect become the last day left, so it would not be a surprise on that day either. The logic continues right back to Monday. Thus an unexpected gift is impossible.

Are there any other ways of solving the paradox?

At first, when you read the paradox with a clear mind, you may think the argument propounded ridiculous. But, like all good paradoxes, it is designed to confuse, and the more you think about it the more unclear your mind is likely to become about it.

12 The following set of dissection puzzles is selected to test your creative skills in cutting up objects and reassembling them into different shapes. The difficulty increases progressively.

(i) Trace the hexagon onto a piece of cardboard and cut along the lines shown. Then reassemble the five pieces into a perfect square.

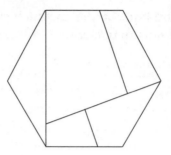

(ii) Reassemble the seven pieces of the star into a hexagon.

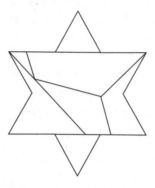

(iii) Make two further cuts of equal length in order to divide the star into five pieces which can then be assembled to form an equilateral triangle.

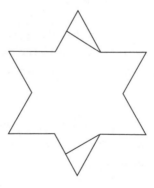

(iv) Cut the square into five pieces which can be reassembled into an octagon.

A hint is provided on page 102.

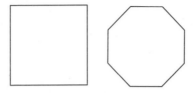

(v) Cut the Latin cross into five pieces and reassemble them to form a square.

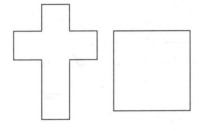

Memory

Memory is the process of storing and retrieving information in the brain. It is this process of memory that is central to learning and thinking.

While very little is known about the mechanics of memory, it is accepted that the more you use it, the better it becomes.

Four different types of remembering are distinguished by psychologists: recollection, recall, recognition and relearning. The first three are self-explanatory while the fourth, relearning, may show evidence of memory in that material that is familiar is often easier to learn a second time round than it would be if it were unfamiliar.

Memory can be broadly divided into three parts, immediate, short term and long term.

Immediate memory is of present occurrences such as noises and events that are seen as pictures in your mind. Many of these are irrelevant and are soon forgotten.

Short-term memory involves events that are stored for future reference such as meetings to be held and tasks that have to be completed in the near future.

Long-term memory involves things like telephone numbers, holiday plans, names and addresses, and memories evoked from the past.

While little is known about the physiology of memory storage in the brain, some researchers suggest that memories are stored in specific sites, and others that memories involve widespread brain regions working together. It is also thought that different storage mechanisms exist for short-term and long-term memories and that if memories are never transferred from the former to the latter they will be lost forever.

Within the brain the limbic system has different memory functions. Animal studies suggest that one circuit through the hippocampus and thalamus may be involved in spatial memories, whereas another circuit, through the amygdala and thalamus, may be responsible for our emotional memories.

Research also suggests that skill memories are stored differently in the brain to intellectual memories.

It is also believed that every picture formed in the brain by sight or thought is stored in the form of a tracing, similar to a negative, that can be recalled at a moment's notice. Thus every incident in a lifetime has been stored, sometimes for only a moment and then discarded. Sometimes even events of no significance can leave a deep impression and be recalled in a flash.

What is accepted, however, is that while it is impossible to improve on past memories, it is possible to improve one's memory for the present and future by practising active recall during learning, by periodic reviews of the material, and by overlearning the material beyond the point of mastery. In addition, there is the technique of mnemonics, which involve the use of associations and various devices to remember particular facts.

The tests which follow are not only to test your powers of memory but to assist you in improving your memory by developing your powers of concentration and to discipline yourself to fix your mind on the subject being studied.

Memory tests

1 Study these figures and numbers for 20 seconds, then turn to page 32 after an interval of 2 minutes and answer the questions.

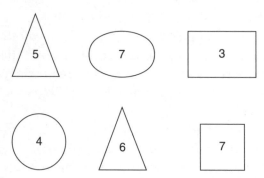

2 Study the set of figures below for 20 seconds, then turn to page 32 after an interval of 3 minutes and answer the question.

3 Study the set of figures and numbers for 2 minutes then turn immediately to page 32 and answer the questions.

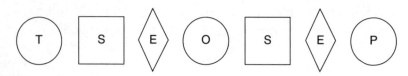

4 This exercise tests your ability to remember pairs of words and form associations. Study the 12 pairs of words for 15 minutes and use your imagination to link each pair of words in as many ways as possible. Then turn to page 32 and answer the questions.

CHEESE	APPLE	MINEFIELD
BRUSH	TELEPHONE	COTTON
TREE	BUTTERCUP	WATER
HANDCUFFS	BRIEFCASE	BOOK
POST	FIELD	YACHT
BALLOON	THORN	CHAIR
VASE	WINDMILL	BRICK
NEEDLE	SAND	ZEBRA

5 Study the figures below for 15 seconds then turn to page 34 immediately and answer the question.

6 Study the following for 2 minutes then turn to page 34 and answer the questions.

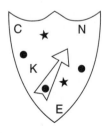

7   Study the following for 20 seconds then turn to page 35 and answer the questions.

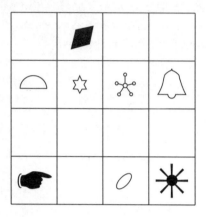

8   Attempt to memorise the following in 60 seconds then turn away and after a 60-second interval turn to page 35 and answer the questions.

> The Lord's Prayer is 66 words, the Gettysburg Address is 286 words, there are 1322 words in the Declaration of Independence, but government regulations on the sale of cabbage total 26,911 words.   *National Review*

9   Study the following for 90 seconds. After an interval of 2 minutes turn to page 36 and answer the question.

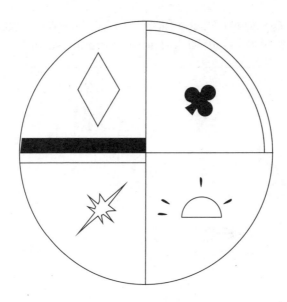

10 Study the array of numbers for 1 minute then turn
immediately to page 36 and answer the question.

8	2	4	1	3	5
	8			7	
	7			9	
	5			4	
3	7	9	4	2	8
	9			8	

11 Here are 20 everyday objects. Study them for 3 minutes then turn to page 36 and answer the question.

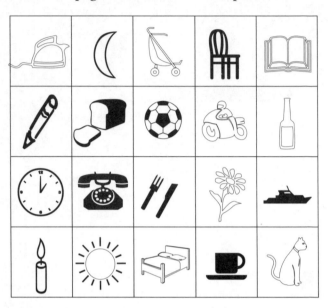

12 Attempt to memorise as many of these 50 words as you can in 5 minutes, then turn to page 37 and answer the questions.

ANIMAL	BIRD	FRUIT	VEGETABLE	COIN
Llama	Sparrow	Orange	Pea	Franc
Tiger	Chaffinch	Apple	Bean	Piastra
Elephant	Emu	Pear	Carrot	Nickel
Cow	Robin	Grape	Swede	Tical
Fox	Lark	Banana	Onion	Lira

FISH	INSECT	FLOWER	COLOUR	GEM
Herring	Bee	Aster	Red	Diamond
Salmon	Ladybird	Daisy	Green	Sapphire
Cod	Ant	Rose	Blue	Emerald
Plaice	Mosquito	Violet	Purple	Pearl
Minnow	Dragon-fly	Wallflower	Mauve	Onyx

13 Study the following shapes for 5 minutes then turn to
page 37 and answer the questions.

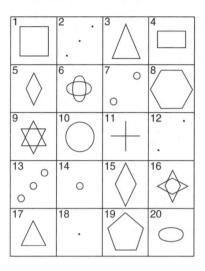

14 Journey

I drove down the road in my car, a Rover, year
M, number 387 NKM. At the traffic lights the
lights were yellow/green. I passed a shop
called Hammond which sold pianos, then I
passed an Esso petrol pump. I went under a
road bridge which had a sign saying max.
height 14ft 6in.

I then passed a clump of elm trees and arrived
at a public house, 'The Black Bear'. The
landlord's name was Robinson. I went in and
ordered an orange juice, which cost £1.19,
then I had a lunch of shepherd's pie, which
cost £6.25.

I came out of the public house and walked to
the car park, where there was a red Post Office
van, number K691 CVB.

There were 17 cars in the car park, and a white van, year K.

Turn to page 38 and answer the questions.

15 Study the babies for 3 minutes then turn to page 39 and answer the questions.

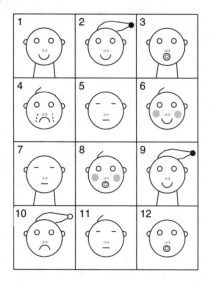

16 Study the following numbers for 5 minutes then turn to page 39 and answer the questions.

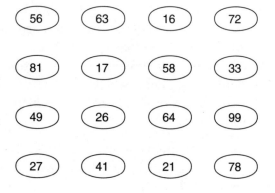

17 Cruise

I was on a cruise ship called 'The Lucine Bill' sailing from the Bahamas to the West Indies.

The ship carried 349 passengers and 117 staff, the weather was fine and we were followed for a short while by 8 porpoises.

As we approached the shore, we could see the spindrift on the tops of the waves. Our hotel in the West Indies was called the 'Orinoco' and the driveway had 28 palm trees flanking the route. There were 16 floors in the hotel and it could cater for 640 guests. The cruise holiday cost $1,800 for each person and lasted for 16 days.

On the first day 128 of us went on a tour of the island, which had a population of 6,500 in 6 towns.

Turn to page 40 and answer the questions.

Questions

1 (i) Which figure appears twice?

   (ii) Which number appears twice?

2 Draw the figure which appears twice in the set.

3 (i) The letter E appears in which figure twice?

   (ii) What word is spelled out by the letters in the three circles?

   (iii) What letter appears in the two squares?

   (iv) What letter appears exactly in the middle of the row?

4 FIELD ....

   APPLE ....

   BRICK ....

   TREE ....

   BALLOON ....

   BUTTERCUP ....

   HANDCUFFS ....

   NEEDLE ....

   ZEBRA ....

   MINEFIELD ....

BOOK ....

CHEESE ....

SAND ....

TELEPHONE ....

WATER ....

YACHT ....

BRUSH ....

WINDMILL ....

POST ....

THORN ....

CHAIR ....

COTTON ....

BRIEFCASE ....

VASE ....

Put the letter A against one pair, the letter B against a second
pair etc., through to the letter L, until you have matched
what you think are the original 12 pairs of words.

5   Which of the following have you just looked at?

(a)

(b)

(c)

(d)

(e)

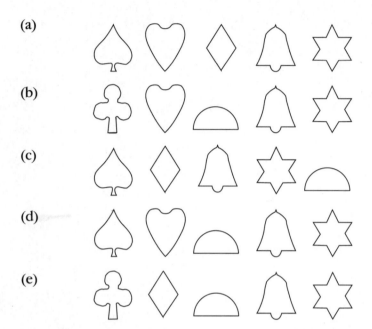

6   (a) How many black dots appear on the shield?

   (b) To which letter is the arrow pointing?

   (c) What word is spelled out by the letters shown on the shield?

   (d) How many stars appear on the shield?

   (e) What letter is in the top left-hand corner of the shield?

7

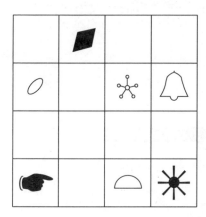

(a) Which two symbols have changed places?

(b) Which symbol is missing from the grid?

8 Fill in the numbers:

The Lord's Prayer is — — — — words, the Gettysburg Address is — — — — words, there are — — — — words in the Declaration of Independence, but government regulations on the sale of cabbage total — — — — words.

9

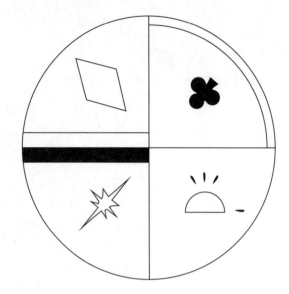

The figure has changed in four ways. Can you list the four ways?

10 Which line of numbers is repeated both horizontally and vertically?

(a) 413794

(b) 379428

(c) 287579

(d) 757942

(e) 875794

11 Write down as many of the 20 objects as you can remember.

12 Name an animal and a fish beginning with C.

Name a bird and a coin beginning with L.

Name a fish and a colour beginning with P.

Name an insect and a gem beginning with D.

Name a fruit and a flower beginning with A.

Name a colour and an insect beginning with M.

Name a fruit and a colour beginning with B.

Name a bird and a vegetable beginning with S.

Name a coin and an animal beginning with F.

Name a colour and a fruit beginning with G.

Name a flower and a bird beginning with R.

Name a coin and an animal beginning with T.

Name a vegetable and a gem beginning with O.

Name a bird and an animal beginning with E.

13 (i) In which square is the hexagon?

(ii) Which shape is in the top right-hand corner?

(iii) Which shape is between the small diamond and the large diamond?

(iv) In which square is the single dot?

(v) Which shape is between the square and the isosceles triangle?

(vi) Which shape is in square 15?

(vii) Which shape is in the bottom left-hand corner?

(viii)   Which square has three small circles?

(ix)   Which shape has two ovals?

(x)   Which square has a cross?

14 (i)   What year was the Post Office van?

(ii)   What did I have for lunch?

(iii)   I passed under a bridge. What was its maximum height for vehicles?

(iv)   What did the shop sell?

(v)   How many cars were there in the car park?

(vi)   What make of car was I driving?

(vii)   What type of trees did I pass?

(viii) What was the name of the pub's landlord?

(ix)   What did the traffic light show?

(x)   What was the shop owner's name?

(xi)   What year was the van in the car park?

(xii)   What was the name of the public house?

(xiii) Who owned the petrol pump?

(xiv)   What was the registration number of the vehicle in the car park?

(xv)   How much did my drink cost?

(xvi)   What was the number of my car?

(xvii) How much did my meal cost?

(xviii) What year was my car?

(xix)   What colour was the van in the car park?

(xx)   What drink did I order?

15 (i)   How many babies are wearing a hat?

(ii)   How many babies have no hair?

(iii)   How many babies have big ears?

(iv)   How many babies are smiling?

(v)   How many babies are asleep?

(vi)   How many babies are crying?

(vii)   How many babies are wearing a bib?

(viii)   How many babies have a dummy?

(ix)   How many babies have hair?

(x)   How many babies are frowning?

(xi)   How many babies are unhappy?

(xii)   How many babies have rosy cheeks?

16 (i)   Name the four corner numbers.

(ii)   How many numbers are there which have the same digit repeated?

(iii)   How many square numbers are there?

(iv)   How many odd numbers are there?

(v)   How many numbers are between 50 and 60?

(vi)   What is the highest number?

(vii)   What is the lowest number?

(viii) Which digit appears most times?

(ix) How many pairs of numbers are one different?

(x) Which number's digits add up to 10?

(xi) How many cube numbers are there?

(xii) How many 7s are there?

17 (i) How many floors did the hotel have?

(ii) What could we see on the waves?

(iii) How much did the cruise cost?

(iv) Where did we sail from?

(v) How many staff were on the ship?

(vi) How many went on the tour?

(vii) What was our destination?

(viii) How many palm trees were in the driveway?

(ix) What were we followed by?

(x) How long was the holiday?

(xi) What was the name of the cruise ship?

(xii) How many guests could the hotel cater for?

(xiii) How many passengers did the ship carry?

(xiv) What was the name of our hotel?

(xv) How many towns did the island have?

(xvi) What was the population of the island?

Mindstretchers

Apart from their recreational value puzzles are a great way of limbering up the brain and exercising the old grey matter. The best puzzles are ones that do not involve any specialised knowledge. In other words, each one of us is capable of solving the puzzle from within our own raw brainpower and is not at an advantage by knowing some specific formula. A typical example of such a puzzle is the following:

> You type four envelopes and four letters. You place the letters in the envelopes at random. What are the chances that only three letters are in their correct envelopes?

At first glance this may appear to be a very difficult puzzle to solve, involving a certain knowledge of probability formulas. This, however, is not the case as with pure logical reasoning each one of us is capable of finding the correct answer.

The answer is, in fact, that the chance of just three being in their correct envelopes is zero. If you have placed three correctly, there is only one envelope left for the fourth letter, and this must be the correct one.

Of course, there is a subtle difference between puzzles and problems. A puzzle is set by another person, and it has a solution which is already known to that person. It is a puzzle, for example, to ask a question such as 'what number is 35 less than six times itself?', or to ask someone to rearrange the letters of the word *chesty* into another word in the English language.

A problem, on the other hand, arises in life. It is not set artificially and there is not an answer already known to someone else. There is no right answer; some solutions may be better than others.

While both puzzles and problems bring their rewards, some may prefer one to the other. Certainly the successful solution of a problem achieves a worthwhile goal, and perhaps the major benefit to be obtained from tackling puzzles is that they stretch and exercise the mind and enable you to tackle the real problems of life with renewed vigour and confidence.

In this section we present a selection of 50 brainteasers, which involve different kinds of thought processes. For the more difficult puzzles, hints are provided and full detailed explanations, where appropriate, are provided with the answers.

Before tackling this selection you may wish to consider the following two brainteasers as examples of the thought processes necessary to solve such puzzles.

Example 1:
My wife usually leaves work at 4.30 p.m., calls at the supermarket, then catches the 5 p.m. train, which arrives at our home town at 5.30 p.m. I leave home each day, drive to the station and pick up my wife at 5.30 p.m., just as she gets off the train. One day last week my wife was able to finish work about five minutes earlier than usual, decided to go straight to the station instead of calling at the supermarket and managed to catch the 4.30 p.m. train, which arrived at our home town station at 5 p.m. Because I was not there to

pick her up she began to walk home. I left home at the usual time, saw my wife walking, turned round, picked her up and drove home, arriving there 12 minutes earlier than usual. For how long did my wife walk before I picked her up?

Solution:
24 minutes

Explanation:
There are two simple formulas for working out the answer to this puzzle.

(i) Total time difference, 30 minutes, less time saved, 12 minutes, is 18 minutes, plus one half time saved, which is 6 minutes, = 24 minutes

(ii) Subtract one half time saved, 6 minutes, from total time difference, 30 minutes, = 24 minutes.

It does not matter, however, if you do not know these formulas as the puzzle can be solved by logic. As I leave according to my usual schedule, we know it is before 5.30 p.m., when I usually pick up my wife. Because we have saved 12 minutes, that must be the same time that it takes me to drive from the point I picked her up, to the station, and back to that same point. Assuming it takes an equal 6 minutes each way I have, therefore, picked up my wife 6 minutes before I would normally do so, which means 5.24 p.m. So my wife must have walked from 5 p.m. to 5.24 p.m., or for 24 minutes.

Example 2:
A woman has two children: what are the odds that both are boys?

Solution:
25%

Explanation:

The simple formula for working this out is .50 × .50 = .25, or 25%.

Again, however, this same formula can be arrived at by pure logic as follows:

Try setting up a tree diagram:

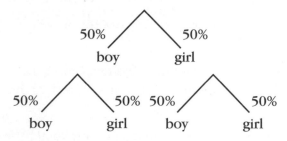

To find out the odds, just multiply across the path that leads to two boys:

.50 × .50 = .25 or 25%.

Had you wanted to know the odds of a boy and a girl, you multiply across the path that leads to a boy and a girl and then add that to the path that leads to a girl and then a boy. They both satisfy the criteria so you add them up.

These two examples will, hopefully, give you some understanding of the type of thinking necessary to arrive at a solution and demonstrate that often there are several different ways of arriving at the same solution.

Puzzles

1 Move the position of just one word to make this sequence alphabetical.

appraisal, absorb, explicit, publish, ironic, arboreal

2   A walker sets off one morning at 6 a.m. to walk to a hotel at the top of a mountain. She arrives at the hotel at 6 p.m. that same day and stays overnight in the hotel. The next morning she sets off back along exactly the same route at 6 a.m. and arrives at the bottom, her original starting point, at 6 p.m.

Is there any point along her route where she arrives at *exactly* the same point at *exactly* the same time during both journeys.

Is there sufficient evidence to determine this fact? Either way, what is your reasoning?

A hint is provided on page 102.

3   Can you draw the figure which should appear instead of the question mark?

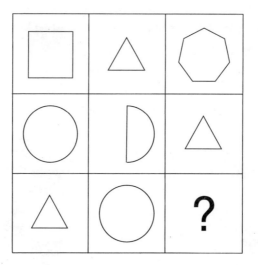

A hint is provided on page 102.

4 Which of these numbers is the odd one out?

79316   64256

         29116

45180   82246

         51204   32128

5 A man is walking his dog on the lead towards home at a steady 3 m.p.h. When they are 7 miles from home the man lets his dog off the lead. The dog immediately runs off towards home at 8 m.p.h. When the dog reaches the house it turns round and runs back to the man at the same speed. When it reaches the man it turns back for the house. This is repeated until the man gets home and lets the dog into the house. How many miles does the dog cover from being let off the lead to being let into the house?

A hint is provided on page 102.

6 Which of these figures is the odd one out?

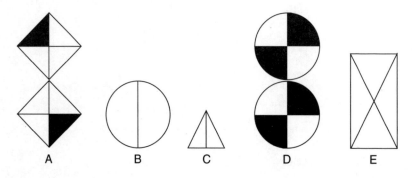

A   B   C   D   E

7   The following words are a logical progression.

THAT
DOCUMENTATION
MEANDER
GRAVY
EMBANKMENT
JUBILEE

What is next – EXTERMINATION, OCCUPATION, GRAMMAR or ZOO?

A hint is provided on page 102.

8   What is the smallest number that will make the following sequence palindromic, i.e. one that will read the same forwards and backwards?

8, 2, 4, 10, 6, 1, 3, ?

A hint is provided on page 102.

9

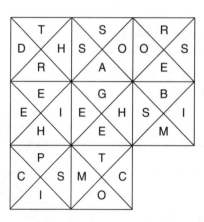

What square below should replace the question mark?

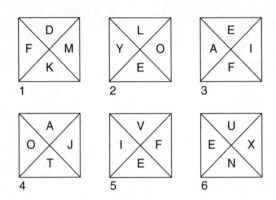

10 Can you say quickly, without putting pen to paper, the sum of all the numbers from 1 to 100 inclusive?

A hint is provided on page 102.

11   14   *   7   4
       *   12   9   16
      10   15   5   13
       6   8   11   *

The numbers 4–16 have already been inserted into the grid, almost, but not quite, at random. Following just two simple rules, where would you place the numbers 1, 2 and 3 in the grid?

12 Calamity Jane hits the target 80 times in 100 shots. Buffalo Bill hits the target 90 times in 100 shots.

What are the chances that the target is hit, if each fires once?

A hint is provided on page 103.

13 What do the following have in common?
      Duke Ellington
      The New Testament
      A red carpet
      The game of Scrabble
      The Morse Code

A hint is provided on page 103.

14

At each stage the black dot moves two places anticlockwise and the white circle moves three places clockwise. After how many moves will both dots be in the same segment?

15 What number is missing from the sequence below?

      523, 212, 917, 151, 311, ? , 531

A hint is provided on page 103.

16 A man jogs at 6 m.p.h. over a certain journey and walks back over the same route at 4 m.p.h. What is his average speed for the journey?

17 What number is missing from the circle?

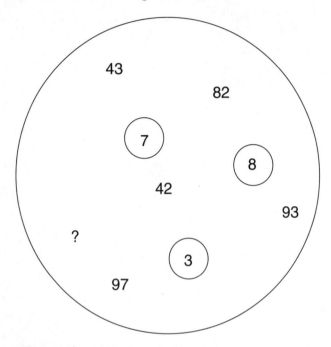

A hint is provided on page 103.

18 Ken and Phil were engaged by the local council to paint lampposts on either side of a street. Ken arrived first and had painted three lampposts on the right-hand side when Phil arrived and pointed out that Ken should be painting the left side. So Ken started afresh on the left side and Phil continued on the right. When Phil had finished his side he went across the street and painted six lampposts for Ken, which finished the job. There were an equal number of lampposts on each side of the street.

Who painted the greater number of lampposts and by how many?

19 abnormal load, make the grade, head teachers

What phrase comes next in the above sequence?

(a) tell the truth

(b) eat humble pie

(c) rags to riches

(d) action replay

(e) do-it-yourself

20 Which is the odd one out?

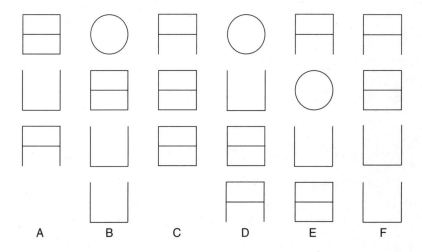

A hint is provided on page 103.

21 Find the product of $(x - a)(x - b)(x - c) \ldots (x - z)$

A hint is provided on page 103.

22 Insert the four missing letters below:

M	S	A	I
D	N	A	U
G	P	V	S
E	I	N	E
I	R	R	G
T	N	F	S
I	T	I	I
S	F	C	I
A	T	E	I
M	C	T	I
I	O	E	A
?	?	?	?
N	S	T	T

A hint is provided on page 103.

23 Which of the following words is the odd one out?

MERIT   BALUSTRADE   BATON   CONTINUITY

RILED   LAMENTABLE   LAIRD   PARAGLIDER

SUMMERTIME   RATED   UNITY   DETER

BLEAT   PRIMORDIAL   EMBITTERED

24 Add two Es to the following group of letters to form another English word.

FAR

The order of the letters can be changed around as you wish.

A hint is provided on page 103.

25 What do the following words have in common?

    ADJOIN
    ATTEND
    GUINEA
    INDEED
    CREAMY
    ASTUTE

26 There was a man in a totally dark room who owned only black or white socks.

In his drawer he had four socks. The chances of him drawing out a pair of white socks was ½. What were the chances of him drawing out a pair of black socks?

A hint is provided on page 103.

27 I was at the golf club and a member had just had a hole in one.

I asked six friends at which hole he had performed this feat. These were their answers. It was an 18-hole course.

A   It was an even number
B   It was an odd number
C   It was a prime number
D   It was a square number
E   It was a cube number
F   It had a one in it

Notes: 1 is not considered to be a prime number
           A square number is 1, 4, 9
           A cube number is 1, 8

I later found out that only one of my friends had told the truth. Which hole was it?

A hint is provided on page 103.

28 There were 19 flautists in an orchestra. One day a consignment of new flutes arrived.

The lead flautist took 1/19th of the total consignment plus 1/19th of a flute.

The second flautist took 1/18th of the remaining consignment plus 1/18th of a flute.

And so on until there were only two flautists left.

The second from last took ½ the remainder and one flute.

The last flautist immediately handed in his resignation. Why?

And how many flutes were delivered?

A hint is provided on page 103.

29 A can mow a field in 6 hours
    B can mow a field in 3 hours
    C can mow a field in 5 hours
    D can mow a field in 10 hours

If they all worked together at their original speeds, how long would it take to mow a field?

A hint is provided on page 104.

30 Clue: ANIMAL FOR THE WINTER? (10)

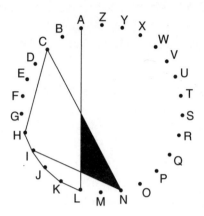

A hint is provided on page 104.

31 'I will bet you £1,' said Bill, 'that if you give me £2, I will give you £3 in return.'

'Done,' replied Alan. Was he?

32 The casino has a roulette wheel with 36 numbers. You choose any 18 numbers and the house has the other 18 numbers. You put $500 into the pool and the bank puts $500 into the pool. If you lose you give the bank half of the money in the pool. If you win you take half of the money in the pool. Is this a fair bet?

A hint is provided on page 104.

33 Which two numbers should replace the two question marks?

5, 3, 7, 6, 7, 3, 3, ?, ?

34 In how many ways may 8 people sit on 8 chairs arranged in a line if 2 of them insist on sitting next to each other?

35 A column was 200 ft high, and its circumference was 16 ft 8 in.

It was wreathed in a spiral garland which passed round it exactly five times. What was the length of this garland in feet and inches?

36 What is unique about the number 854917632?

37 26 cards each bearing a different letter of the alphabet are shuffled and placed on a table. What are the chances of the first three cards turned over being A, B, C, in that order?

38 Write down a 10-digit number such that the first digit indicates the total number of zeros in the number, the second digit indicates the number of ones, and so on to the last digit (zero is a digit).

39 The ten digits 0, 1, 2, 3, 4, 5, 6, 7, 8, 9 can be arranged into numbers and added to equal many totals. Nobody has yet arranged them to equal 1984. However, 9 digits can be arranged to equal 1984.

Which digit has to be omitted?

40 Solve this unusual message.

ZABXG	ILCMD	FAYOK	MCBEO
	QSIUL	NCAPD	FGIAE

41 There are three boxes, labelled WW, BB and WB, but all of the labels have been switched.

> One contains 2 black marbles
> One contains 2 white marbles
> One contains 1 black and 1 white marble

How many marbles must be selected in order to correct the labels?

42 A chambermaid has mixed up the room keys. There are 20 rooms. What is the maximum number of trials required to sort out the keys?

43 There are 100 nuts in five bowls.

> 1st + 2nd = 52
> 2nd + 3rd = 43
> 3rd + 4th = 34
> 4th + 5th = 30

How many nuts are in each bowl?

44 A man went fishing and caught a fish. The man's friend asked him how much it weighed. The man said,

> 'The tail weighs 18 ounces. The head as much as the tail and half the body, and the body weighs as much as the head and tail together.'

How much did the fish weigh?

45 A number of people were surveyed = 300
   Number who drank whisky = 234
   Number who drank gin = 213
   Number who drank both = 144
   Number who drank neither = 0

Find the error in the figures above.

46 Which word should replace the question mark to follow a system?

> STOIC, CLUMP, PRETTY, ?, ALMOST, TUBULAR, RECORD

Choose from: BEAN, PANT, YOGA, SITE, EGOS

47 If you add the square of Tom's age to Molly's age, the sum is 62. If you add the square of Molly's age to the age of Tom, the sum is 176. What were their ages?

48 What do these words have in common?

> REPAST
> HUNGRY
> DEODAR
> STACKED
> STARLIGHT
> MISSAL

49 The temperature at noon for five successive days was different each day and was expressed to the nearest whole number.

Their product = 12°C

What were the five temperatures?

50 Out of 100 ladies surveyed,

> 85 had a white handbag
> 75 had black shoes
> 60 carried an umbrella
> 90 wore a ring

How many ladies at least must have had all four items?

Agility of mind

Agility of mind is the ability to think quickly and react instinctively to certain situations. All the tests in this chapter are speed tests against the clock where not only must you weigh up each situation quickly, but keep your wits about you while under pressure.

A speed test is a general term for any test that measures ability by determining the number of problems that can be dealt with successfully within a fixed time period. Opposite to this is a power test, which measures ability by determining the degree of difficulty of material with no time pressure on the test taker.

The questions in the tests that follow are not in themselves difficult. However, when presented as a series of questions to be attempted within a set time limit, the brain must adapt to the situation before it and agility of mind plus a great deal of concentration is required in order to score highly.

Mental agility tests

1 You have 25 minutes in which to complete the 10 questions, which gradually increase in difficulty.

A	B	C	D	E	
F	G	H	I	J	
K	L	M	N	O	
P	Q	R	S	T	
U	V	W	X	Y	Z

(i)   What letter is two below the letter immediately to the left of the letter three above the letter S?

(ii) What letter is immediately above the letter immediately to the right of the letter two below the letter immediately to the left of the letter L?

(iii) What letter is two to the left of the letter three above the letter immediately above the letter immediately to the left of the letter Z?

(iv) What letter is two to the right of the letter which comes midway between the letters E and U?

(v)   What letter is two above the letter immediately to the left of the letter three below the letter two to the right of the letter F?

(vi) What letter is immediately below the letter which comes midway between the letter immediately below the letter G and the letter immediately above the letter S?

(vii)   What letter is three to the right of the letter immediately below the letter two to the right of the letter two below the letter F?

(viii) What letter is two above the letter immediately to the right of the letter immediately below the letter two to the left of the letter T?

(ix)   What letter is two to the left of the letter immediately below the letter two to the right of the letter which comes midway between the letter immediately to the left of the letter V and the letter two to the left of the letter M?

(x)   What letter is two to the right of the letter three above the letter immediately to the left of the letter immediately above the letter three to the left of the letter Z?

2   In each line of numbers, disregard all the numbers that appear more than once and then write the remaining numbers in reverse order. You have 6 minutes in which to complete the task.

For example: 4723869764 = 9832

(a) 9482374827981   (i) 98243159752168

(b) 4967284317   (j) 29374271824781

(c) 47839274283   (k) 1974384569172

(d) 14631296847235   (l) 861932825786243

(e) 921638427952   (m) 728361751692483

(f) 746983471892   (n) 6379132758462

(g) 1524693521725   (o) 9832176854721638

(h) 743892176521387

3 In each of the following you have to decide which figure in each set is the odd one out. You have 20 minutes in which to complete the test.

For example:

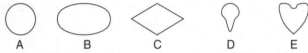

Figure C is the odd one out because it is a straight-sided figure, whereas all the rest have rounded or curved sides.

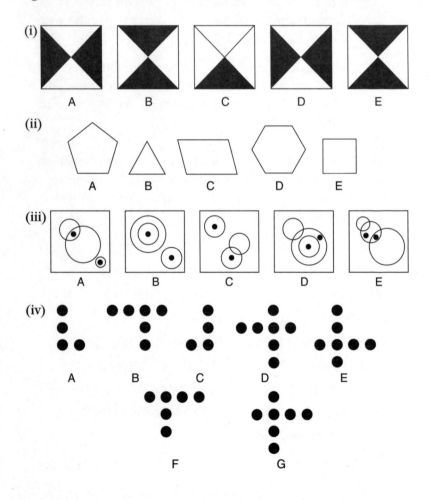

(v)

(vi)

(vii)

(viii)

(ix)

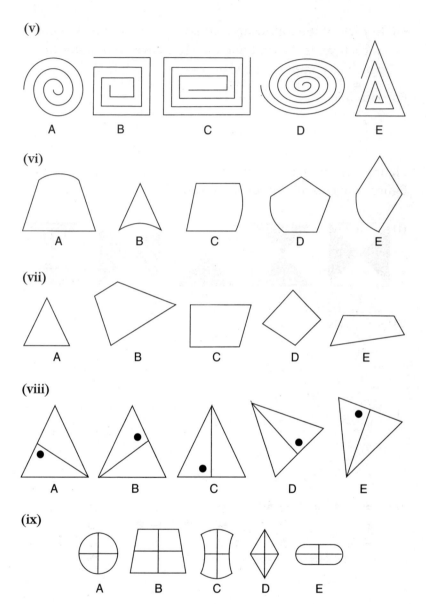

(x)

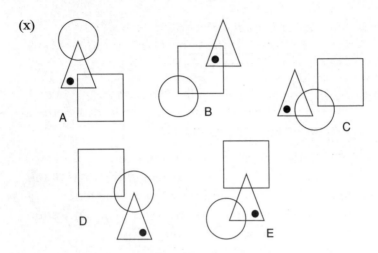

4   In each line of numbers rearrange the digits so that all
the even numbers are in **ascending** order, followed by
all the odd digits in **descending** order. You have 4
minutes in which to complete the test.

For example: 76524 = 24675

(i)   38914   (ix) 9164382

(ii)   85792   (x)   4792631

(iii) 94621   (xi) 8649327

(iv)   647832   (xii) 5921738

(v)   145739   (xiii) 1769842

(vi)   912465   (xiv) 82976354

(vii) 5273819   (xv) 97168325

(viii) 6492153

5   In this test we are testing your ability to juggle with words and fit them into an interlocking grid. You must place all the words in the crossword within 30 minutes to satisfactorily complete the task. Three 3-letter words have already been placed.

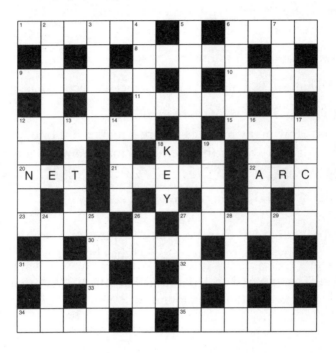

IDEAL	YELLOW	DANCE	ALERT	FAIRLY	
DELTA	LOCAL	NONE	TACIT	EARN	LAGOON
ELEVEN	MADE	AISLE	INTER	NADIR	FENCE
SPONGE	EDIFY	MYNAH	ERASE	REVEAL	ALPHA
STAR	IDIOM	OWNER	LAIR	NEEDY	BLUE
AWASH	RHYME	SEND	HEEL	ABOVE	VALUE

6   The following is a speed test of 10 questions designed to test your powers of mental calculation and logic. In themselves the questions are not particularly difficult but because of the short period of time in which you are allowed to complete the test, alertness and agility of mind are the key ingredients to scoring well, as with all the tests in this section.

You have just 15 minutes in which to complete the 10 questions.

(i)   Which two shapes are identical

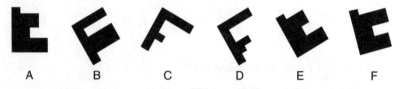

A   B   C   D   E   F

(ii)   When a full barrel contains 90 litres of water, how many litres remain once 60% has been used?

(iii) This box is 1 m × 1 m × 50 cm. How many can be packed into a container 4 m × 3 m × 3 m?

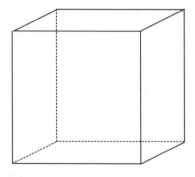

(iv) What is the answer to this calculation?

$1\frac{1}{8} \times \frac{2}{3}$

(v)

What shape below is identical to the shape above?

A   B   C   D   E

(vi) What number is missing?

| 17 | + | ? | ÷ | 3 | = | 11 |

(vii) Which two shapes are identical?

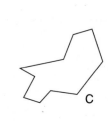

A

B

C

D   E

(viii)

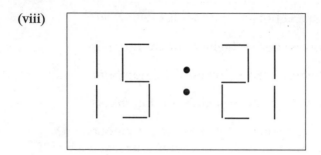

The above is a mirror image of a clock face. What time was it one hour ago?

(ix) How many minutes before 1 a.m. is it if one hour later it will be three times as many minutes after 1 a.m.?

(x) What number continues this sequence?

1, 3, 2, 4, 3, 5, ?

7 Study the numbers in the square then answer the 10 questions. You have 20 minutes in which to complete this task.

Square numbers are 1, 4, 9, 16, 25, 36, 64

Cube numbers are 1, 27, 64

9	42	16	88
83	25	37	23
17	27	39	36
95	64	19	6

Find the total of:

(i)   Lowest odd + highest square numbers

(ii)   Highest even + lowest cube numbers

(iii)   Lowest prime + highest odd numbers

(iv)   Lowest square + lowest even numbers

(v)   Highest even + highest prime numbers

(vi)   Highest cube + lowest prime numbers

(vii) Lowest square + lowest cube numbers

(viii) Lowest odd + highest even numbers

(ix)   Highest prime + highest square numbers

(x)   Highest odd + highest cube numbers

8   Some letters have exposed end points. For example:
    D = 0
    P = 1
    I = 2
    E = 3
    X = 4

Calculate the values of the following. You have 10 minutes.

(i) H + R = ?	(vi) H ÷ V = ?	
(ii) K − I = ?	(vii) U × Z = ?	
(iii) B + L = ?	(viii) E ÷ F = ?	
(iv) A × S = ?	(ix) C × D = ?	
(v) X − P = ?	(x) T − V = ?	

9 Study the crossword then answer the 10 questions. You have 10 minutes.

	C		Z		S		O		S	
C	H	E	E	S	E		D	E	P	U	T	Y
	A		N		D		Y		I	
I	N	K		P	A	R	S	O	N	A	G	E
	D		H		N		S		D		R	
D	E	B	U	T		R	E	F	R	A	I	N
	L		M		D		Y		I		P	
R	I	D	D	L	E	R		O	F	F	E	R
	E		I		L		W		T		W	
P	R	I	N	C	I	P	A	L		H	A	M
			G		G		S		W		T	
H	I	T	E	C	H		T	U	R	R	E	T
			R		T		E		Y		R	

(i)   How many Hs are there?

(ii)   How many nouns are there?

(iii) How many Es are there?

(iv)   How many Ys are there?

(v)   How many six-letter words are there?

(vi)   How many hyphenated words are there?

(vii) How many Rs are there?

(viii) How many 10-letter words are there?

(ix)   How many Zs are there?

(x)   How many five-letter words are there?

10 This is a magic word square. Each words spells the same
across and down. Each letter has a grid reference. For
example, C = 4G and 7D. Study the grid then answer the
10 questions. You have 5 minutes.

	A	B	C	D	E	F	G
1	P	R	E	P	A	R	E
2	R	E	M	O	D	E	L
3	E	M	U	L	A	T	E
4	P	O	L	E	M	I	C
5	A	D	A	M	A	N	T
6	R	E	T	I	N	U	E
7	E	L	E	C	T	E	D

Write down all of the grid references for the 10 letters
below.

(i)   D   (vi)   U

(ii) O   (vii) M

(iii) T   (viii) P

(iv) L   (ix)   I

(v)   E   (x)   N

Intelligence tests

Intelligence is the capacity to learn or understand. Every one of us possesses a single general ability of mind. This general ability varies in amount from person to person, but remains approximately the same throughout life for any individual. It is this ability which enables each of us to deal with real situations and profit intellectually from sensory experience.

In psychology, intelligence is defined as the capacity to acquire knowledge and understanding and use it in different novel situations. Under test conditions it is possible to study formally the success of an individual in adapting to a specific situation.

Any test that purports to measure intelligence is, by definition, an IQ test. Such tests usually consist of a graded series of tasks, each of which has been standardised with a large representative section of the population.

The letters IQ stand for Intelligence Quotient. The word quotient means the results of dividing one quantity by another. It is generally accepted that a person's IQ rating is a hereditary characteristic and barely changes throughout life in adults. Up to the age of adulthood, mental age remains fairly constant in development to about the age of 13, after which it is shown to slow up, and beyond the age of 18 little or no improvement is found.

When measuring the IQ of a child, the child would attempt an intelligence test that has been standardised, with an average score recorded for each age group. Thus a child of 10 years of age who scored the results expected of a child of 12 would have an IQ calculated as follows:

$$\frac{\text{mental age}}{\text{chronological age}} \times 100 = \text{IQ rating}$$

$$\frac{12 \text{ years old}}{10 \text{ years old}} \times 100 = 120 \text{ IQ rating}$$

This method would not, however, apply to adults, who have to be judged on an IQ test whose average score is 100 and their results graded above and below this norm according to known scores, the distribution of IQ to the population taking the form of a fairly regular bell curve.

While it is generally agreed that IQ is hereditary and remains fairly constant throughout life, it is possible to improve your own performance on IQ tests. It is this improvement in performance that the authors set out to achieve in several of their books.

IQ tests are set and used on the assumption that those taking the test have no knowledge of the testing method itself and that they know very little about the question methods within these tests. It follows, therefore, that if you learn something about this form of testing and know how to approach the different kinds of questions you can improve your performance on the tests themselves.

This chapter consists of two separate IQ tests each of 40 questions. Within each of these tests are four sub-tests, each of 10 questions, in four different disciplines: spatial ability, logical thought processes, verbal ability and numerical ability. It is these disciplines that are most common in IQ testing.

Because these tests have been specially compiled for this book and have not, therefore been standardised, an actual IQ rating cannot be given. We do, however, give a performance rating for each subset of 10 questions to enable you to identify your own strengths or weaknesses, and we also give an overall rating for each complete test of 40 questions. It is this overall rating which is the best guide to your IQ rating.

10-question test (time limit 30 minutes):

10	exceptional
8–9	excellent
7	very good
5–6	good
4	average

40-question test (time limit 2 hours):

36–40	exceptional
31–35	excellent
25–30	very good
19–24	good
14–18	average

IQ test one

Spatial ability test
Read the instruction to each question and study each set of diagrams carefully.

1   Which is the odd one out?

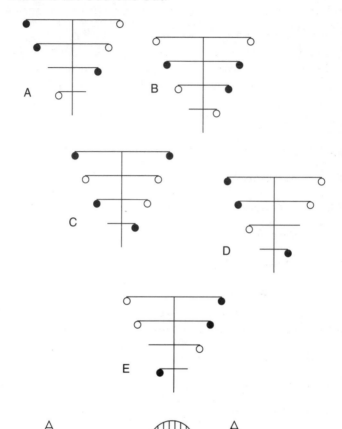

2

What comes next in the above sequence?

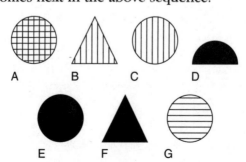

3

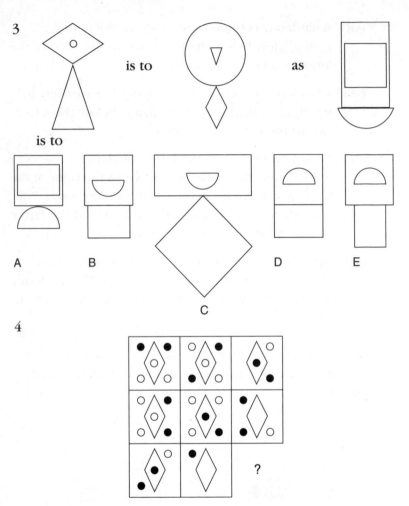

is to

as

is to

A   B   D   E

C

4

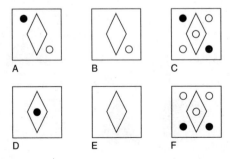

What square should replace the question mark?

A   B   C

D   E   F

5

What comes next in the above sequence?

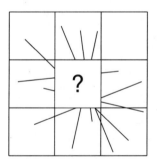

6

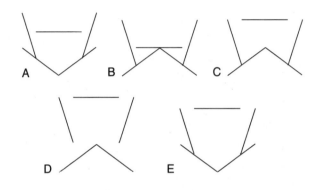

Which square should replace the question mark so that all lines become continuous?

A   B   C   D   E   F

7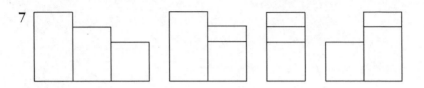

What comes next in the above sequence?

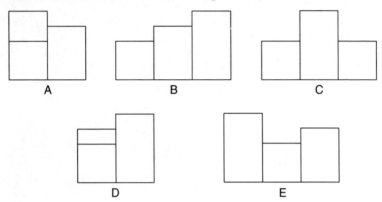

8 Which is the odd one out?

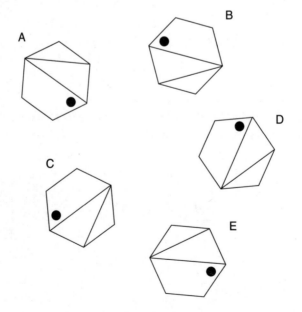

9

What comes next in the above sequence?

| A | B | C | D | E |

10

   is to

as

is to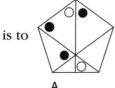

| A | B | C | D |

Logic test

1   What letters should replace the question marks?

G	B	F	G	A	F	N	A	C	N
F	K	A	B	N	G	C	F	K	A
A	C	N	K	C	B	K	G	B	F
N	N	C	C	K	K	B	B	G	G
C	A	K	?	?	C	G	K	F	B
K	F	B	?	?	N	F	C	A	K
B	G	G	F	F	A	A	N	N	C
G	B	F	G	A	F	N	A	C	N
F	K	A	B	N	G	C	F	K	A
A	C	N	K	C	B	K	G	B	F

2   379642 is to 627493

     as 847346 is to :   a) 436478
                             b) 364748
                             c) 346487
                             d) 364478
                             e) 463478

3   Alan beats Tom at tennis but loses to Hazel. Kathy usually
wins against Tom, sometimes against Alan, but never
against Hazel. Who is the weakest player?

4   What numbers are missing from the grid?

4	3	8	7	5	6
2	5	7	6	8	5
7	8	1	8	7	6
5	4	7	6	4	8
3	8	6	3	?	7
7	2	5	8	?	4

5   SCEPTICAL, ASPECTUAL, INSPECTOR, PROSPECTS

Which word comes next in the above sequence?

CRESCENTS, WINDSWEPT, BOLSHEVIST, ABASEMENT, CARBUNCLE

6   Where should the hands point on the fourth clock face?

7 Which letters should replace the question mark?

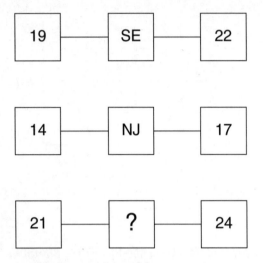

8 Which set of letters is the odd one out?

KMQO   LNRP   CEJH

MOSQ   BDHF

SUYW

9 What number should replace the question mark?

63 : 396

42 : 264

81 : ?

10 A ball is put in an empty bag. You do not know whether the ball is black or white. A second ball, which you know to be black, is then put in the bag. A ball is then drawn out, and it proves to be black.

What are the chances that the ball remaining in the bag is also black?

Verbal ability test

1　Which three-letter word can be placed behind each of the following to form four- and five-letter words?

    P
    ME
    SC   * * *
    W
    R

2　Which is the odd one out?

METONOMY, MONTAGE, ANTITHESIS, EPITHET, ASSONANCE

3　OBESE REDCOATS

is an anagram of which two words (8,5) that are opposite in meaning?

4　Which two words below are closest in meaning?

RELIGIOUS, MONASTIC, CHORAL, AUSTERE, MASTERLY

5　The name of which precious stone can be placed on the bottom line to complete eight 3-letter words reading downwards?

P	R	P	M	A	B	H	S
E	I	I	E	S	U	A	A
*	*	*	*	*	*	*	*

6   OHM:ELECTRICITY

Choose the pair that best expresses a relationship similar to the pair above.

   a) BAR:TEMPERATURE

   b) WATT:POWER

   c) JOULE:PRESSURE

   d) FARAD:RADIATION

   e) ERG:PRESSURE

7

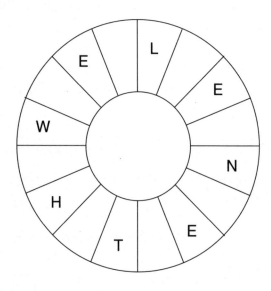

Read clockwise to find a 16-letter phrase. Only alternate letters are shown.

8   The following clue leads to which pair of rhyming words?

   SCRUTINISED ESCORT

9   The following is extracted from which hyphenated word?

   * * * O D - C U * * * * * *

   Clue: terror

10   Place two letters in each pair of parentheses so that they
   finish the word on the left and start the word on the
   right. Reading downwards, combine these pairs to spell
   out a six-letter word.

   MO (**) EN

   CO (**) ST

   NE (**) OM

Numerical ability test

1   What number should replace the question mark?

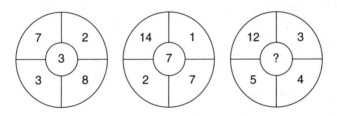

2   What number should replace the question mark?

3   What number should replace the question mark?

   742 (7390) 316
   219 (7148) 527
   316 (?   ) 431

4 100, 99.5, 98.5, 97, 95, ?

   What number comes next?

5 A train travelling at a speed of 40 m.p.h. enters a tunnel
   that is 1.25 miles long. The length of the train is 0.25
   miles. How long does it take for all of the train to pass
   through the tunnel, from the moment the front enters to
   the moment the rear emerges?

6 What number should replace the question mark?

7 What number should replace the question mark?

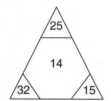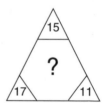

8 What number should replace the question mark?

   53 (3) 59
   71 (9) 79
   29 (?) 98

9 1, 2, 5, 14, 41, ?

   What number comes next?

10 What number should replace the question mark?

689 : 39
743 : 25
497 : ?

IQ test two

Spatial ability test

1

What comes next in the above sequence?

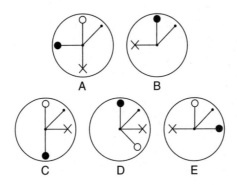

2   Which is the odd one out?

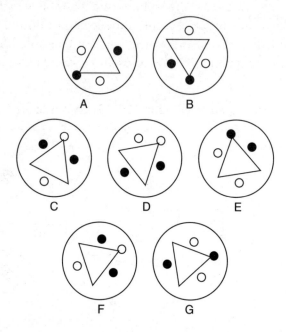

3   Each of the nine squares in the grid marked 1A to 3C
    should incorporate all the lines and symbols which are
    shown in the squares of the same letter and number
    immediately above and to the left. For example, 2B
    should incorporate all the lines and symbols that are in 2
    and B.

    One of the squares is incorrect. Which one is it?

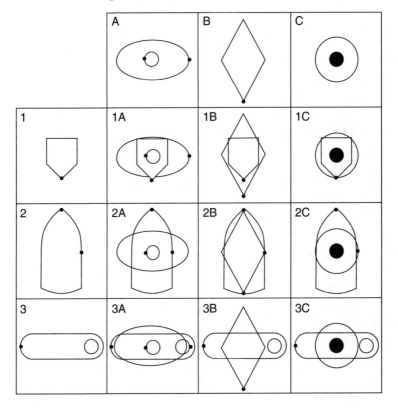

4

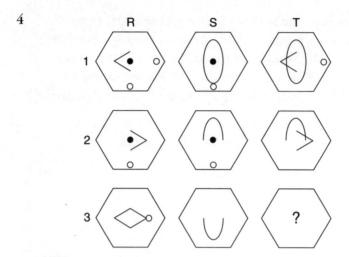

Which hexagon should replace the question mark?

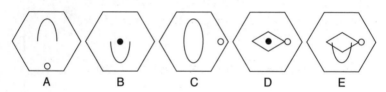

5

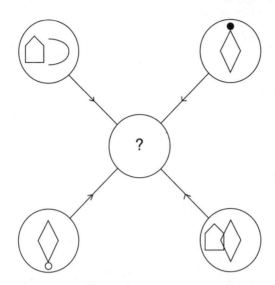

Each line and symbol which appears in the four outer circles, above, is transferred to the centre circle according to these rules:

If a line or symbol occurs in the outer circles:

Once:	it is transferred
Twice:	it is possibly transferred
Three times:	it is transferred
Four times:	it is not transferred

Which of the circles shown below should appear at the centre of the diagram, above?

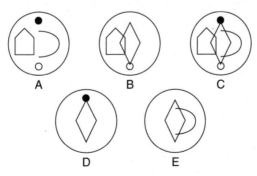

6

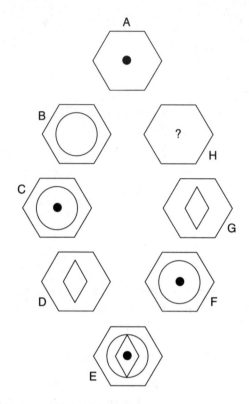

Which hexagon should replace H?

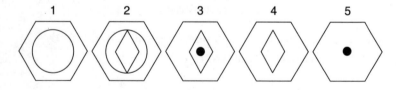

7

X

Which of the five boxes below has the most in common with the box above, marked X?

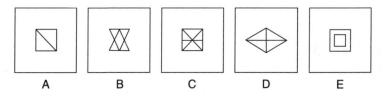

A   B   C   D   E

8

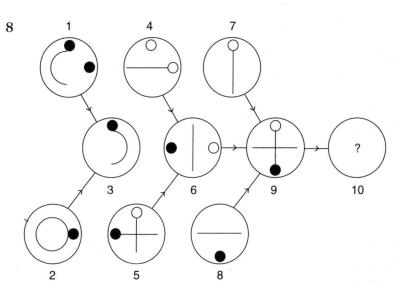

Which circle should replace 10?

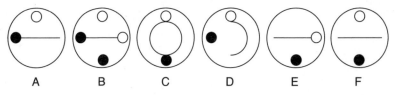

A   B   C   D   E   F

9

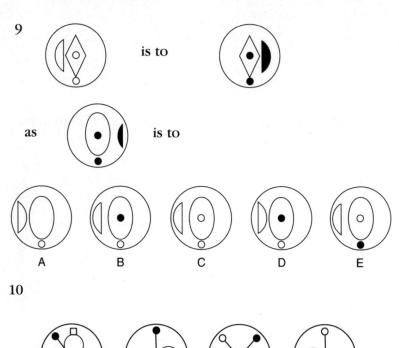

10

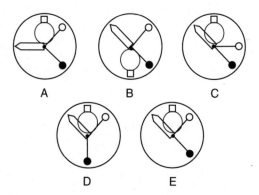

What comes next in the above sequence?

Logic test

1   There are four towns and a new road system has to
     connect all four towns. It is essential to spend the
     minimum by reducing the road mileage. What is the best
     method?

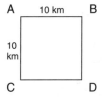

     One solution = 40 km. Can you find one better?

2   A shopkeeper had some scales weighing up to 40 kg.
     What value weights would be needed to weigh any
     amount of whole kilograms up to 40 kg?

3   I have two standard 6-sided dice. What are the chances
     that with one roll I can score 9 or more?

4   At the bridge table, which is more likely – that a pair of
     players will have no diamonds dealt to them, or all of the
     diamonds dealt to them?

5   A boy will be 8 years old on his 1st birthday. How will
    that be?

6

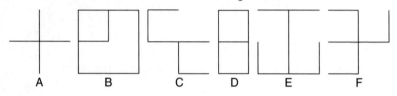

What comes next in the above sequence?

A   B   C   D   E   F

7   If you make a random number out of a long list of digits
    such as:

    1 7 2 5 9 0 6 6 4 3 2 1 8 8 7 6

    What is the average difference between two digits?

    Is it $\dfrac{0 + 9}{2} = 4{\cdot}5$?

8   What is the value of

    $9 - 9 + 9 - 9 + 9 - 9 + 9 - 0 \longrightarrow \infty$?

9 Seven people were sitting around a table. In how many different ways can they be arranged?

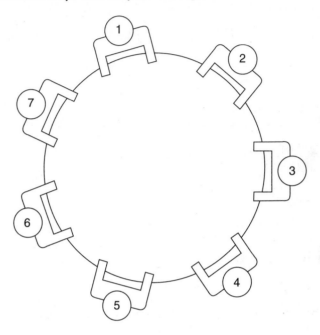

10 Four standard dice are stacked up. What is the total of the seven top and bottom faces that are hidden?

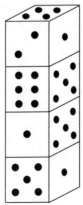

Verbal ability test

1   Fill in the missing letters to find two words which are synonyms.

2   What is the name given to a group of FORESTERS?

    a) STRIP
    b) BRANCH
    c) STALK
    d) BAND
    e) GREENHEART

3   What is a FOSS?

    a) MOSS
    b) A CASTLE
    c) A HILL
    d) A DITCH
    e) A WALL

4   Insert a word in the brackets which completes the first word and starts the second word.

    MUD (. . . .) SPUR

5   Which of the following is not a CLOTH?

    a) HESSIAN
    b) MARCASITE
    c) TAFFETA
    d) CORDUROY
    e) ORGANDIE

6 Travel from circle to circle only along the lines, and, using each circle only once, spell out a ten-letter word.

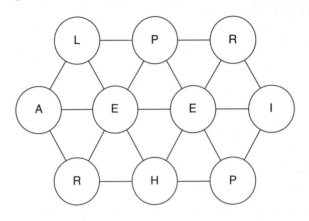

7 Which word means the same as OBEISANCE?

LIKING, PENURY, HOMAGE, SLAVERY, SLACKNESS, FORGETFUL

8 PANTOMIME is to HARLEQUIN as CIRCUS is to:

a) FUNAMBULIST
b) CHOIR MASTER
c) SKYLARKER
d) PROMENADER
e) CATABAPTIST

9 Which two words are opposite in meaning?

INFIRMITY, ENLARGEMENT, SOOTHING, STRENGTH, FIENDISH, PALTRY

10 Which of the following is not a fruit?

a) WAPWOT
b) ABANAN

c) ECILEH
d) NERGOA
e) GEMTUN

Numerical ability test

1   What number should replace the question mark?

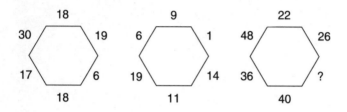

2   What number should replace the question mark?

3   Find the missing number.

4   What number should replace the question mark?

6	18	8	30
7	17	5	18
6	16	9	38
6	10	10	?

5 What number should replace the question mark?

0.67, 0.69, 0.48, 0.88, 0.29, 1.07, ?

6 Simplify

$16 - 7 \times 9 + 4 - 12 \div 4$

7 Simplify

$$\frac{6}{17} \div \frac{24}{34}$$

8 What is the value of $2\frac{1}{4} + 17\frac{7}{8}$?

9 What number should replace the question mark?

10 What number should replace the question mark?

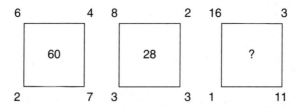

Hints

Creativity

10 One square will consist of one piece only.

Two squares will consist of two pieces each, all four of these pieces being identical.

One square will consist of four identical pieces.

12 (iv) Try creating an internal square.

Mindstretchers

2 Imagine she has a twin brother who does the downward journey on the same day that she does the upward journey.

3 How many sides has each shape?

5 For what length of time does the dog run backwards and forwards?

7 Consider the length of each word.

8 Think about converting the numbers into another form.

10 Think about pairs of numbers.

12 Remember the tree.

13 Look closely at each line. Do you see anything hidden in each?

15 Back to front.

17 Why are the three numbers circled. What is the relationship of the other numbers to the digits 783, or any combination of these digits?

20 Look at this from all sides.

21 What about $(x - x)$?

22 These are crazy columns. Try a bit of column hopping.

24 Read the question very carefully.

26 In a probability puzzle all of the chances must add up to 1. Example: two runners were equal in performance, their chances in a two-person race were A = $\frac{1}{2}$, B = $\frac{1}{2}$. But there was a possibility of a dead-heat, and the chance of a dead-heat was 10 to 1 against. Therefore, their true chances were A = $4\frac{1}{2}/10$, B = $4\frac{1}{2}/10$, dead heat 1/10. Total = 1.

27 Analyse the statements on a chart numbered 1–18. Place a tick against each reply. The number which has only one tick is the answer. If three had told the truth, the number with three ticks would have been the answer.

28 Each member must take a complete flute or flutes. One cannot take a portion of flute.

29 You cannot add them up as you would get 24 hours. You can add up the reciprocals (the number divided into 1).

30 You have to find the letters in the form of an anagram. If a line finishes at a letter, then that letter starts the word or finishes the word.

A then starts or finishes the word. It is not possible in this case to find the other letter.

We know the following letters are in the word:

A C H I N L

J and K might be in the word.

There must be some doubled letters as we have to find 10.

Probably C H I L A.

The second from last letter is possibly L.

H probably is followed by I.

32 Work out how much the bank wins on a winning streak, and how much the punter wins on a winning streak.

Answers

1   Explanations:
(i) Every alternate figure is a
    triangle. In between is a sequence
    of square/circle. The content of
    each square is repeated in the
    next circle.

(ii) Working clockwise, a circle is
     added at each stage. When the
     circle first appears it is half black,
     half white, the right half being
     black. At all subsequent stages the
     circle is fully black.

(iii) Working clockwise, a square is
      added to each side of the
      pentagon in turn. The first time it
      appears, the square is on the
      outside of the pentagon, but then
      it alternates inside/outside at each
      subsequent stage.

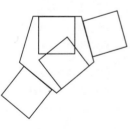

(iv)   The circle/triangle/square are being repeated in the same order. They first appear at the top, then move around clockwise one arm at each stage.

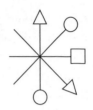

(v)   An additional quarter appears black at each stage. In the first set, the added black quarters appear clockwise, In the second set they are appearing anti-clockwise.

(vi)   The whole figure is rotating 90° clockwise at each stage.

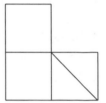

(vii) A smaller half circle is added at each stage, first the left side, then the right side. At the same stage the previous half-circle becomes a full circle.

(viii) At each stage a dot is added, first on the horizontal, then the vertical.

(ix)   At each stage another line is added. At subsequent stages each dot moves from right to left of the line.

(x) At each stage the black dot
    moves one place clockwise, and
    the white dot moves from right
    to left and back again on the
    horizontal line.

Rating:

   10   exceptionally creative
   9   very creative
   7–8 well above average
   5–6 above average
   3–4 average

2 Put three pigs in each of three pens and build a fourth
   pen around the other three.

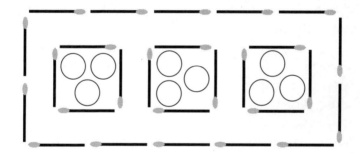

3 Explanations:

(i) The man is a travel agent. He had sold a man two tickets
    for an ocean voyage, one round trip and one one-way.
    The surname of the man who bought the tickets is the
    same as that of the woman who fell overboard and
    drowned in the article he is reading.

(ii) The man has been lost in the desert for days. As there
    were no landmarks he started sticking slips of paper to
    cactus as he passed them. After several days walking with

no water left he comes across a cactus with a piece of paper stuck to it already. Realising he is walking in circles he gives up the ghost and lies down beside the cactus to die.

(iii) He was in an open-top car and was shot through the top with a crossbow.

(iv) He cannot get to sleep because someone in the adjoining room is snoring loudly. He works out the number of the room and makes a telephone call to that room. As soon as the person answers, he puts down the telephone and goes to sleep before the snoring starts again.

(v) The man shaking his foot was leaning against a metal light pole. The other man thought the pole was live and that the man was being electrocuted. The man hits him sharply on the arm to try to free it, breaking the man's arm in the process.

4   Answers:
   1 Royal prerogative
   2 Sitting target
   3 Square deal
   4 Never a cross word
   5 A blot on the horizon
   6 Cross country
   7 Scatterbrain
   8 Change of policy
   9 The height of passion
  10 A state of confusion
  11 Neon light
  12 Snake in the grass

5   As this question is limited only by your own imagination, there are no answers!

6 Scoring and analysis:
   You can mark your efforts yourself, but it is better if you
   get a friend or family member to do so.

Allow:

2 points for any good or original answer
1 point for a good attempt
0 points for completely impractical answers

18–24 points	highly creative
13–17 points	above average
7–12 points	average

7   The logic we have worked to is shown below. Larger
     segments contain circles which alternate black and white
     in adjoining segments. Smaller segments contain
     triangles. Each straight row of triangles alternates black
     and white.
     It may be that you have created a pattern different to the
     one above. Providing this has the same desired symmetry
     throughout it is indeed a valid attempt.

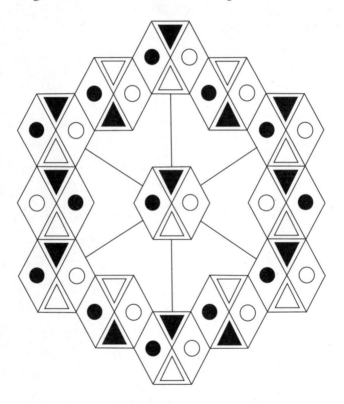

8   Scoring and analysis:

You can mark this test yourself, but it is best marked by a friend or family member.

Award one mark for each recognisable sketch, providing it is not similar to any of the other sketches.

For example, if you draw a face, a second face scores no points as each sketch must have an original theme.

You thus obtain marks for variety. If you are creative you will tend to try to draw something different for each sketch.

There are no correct answer for the six sketches, as for each there is an infinite number of ideas.

Scoring:

6 points	exceedingly creative
4–5	very creative
3	creative
2	average

9

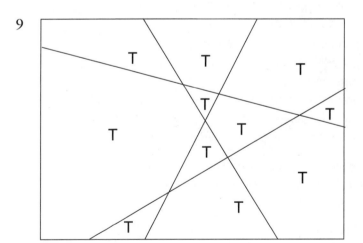

10

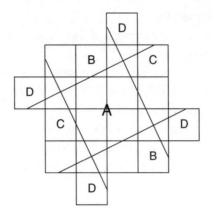

A = one square
B + B = one square
C + C = one square
D + D + D + D = one square

11 The Greek philosopher Zeno suggested that in the last
    few seconds of Thursday you see someone approaching
    with the gift. 'Here is the gift,' he says and looks at his
    very precise watch. You claim it is not unexpected for the
    reasons previously outlined. 'But,' says your friend,
    'Thursday is ending and Friday is about to begin,' and
    hands you the present at the precise instant of the
    change – the moment between Thursday and Friday.

    However, there are other possibilities, perhaps less
    fanciful than that proposed by Zeno, two of which we
    suggest as follows:

    (i) Five boxes are placed in the office. Four have weights
        precisely the same as the present and one contains
        the present. You are to pick one box each day when
        given the word. The gift will, therefore, be

unexpected – unless, of course you haven't picked the correct box by Thursday (when the odds are even) or Friday (when the odds are a certainty).

(ii) A colleague comes to your house on the Saturday or Sunday immediately prior to your last working week and presents you with the gift on one of the very two days you did not expect to receive it.

12 (i)

(ii)

(iii)

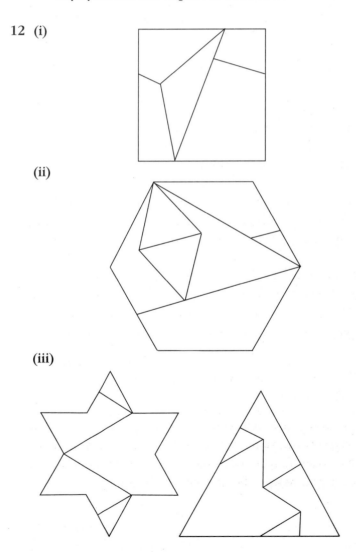

(iv)

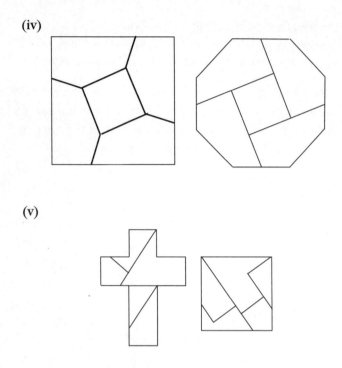

(v)

Mindstretchers

1 Move *publish* between *appraisal* and *absorb*. The first and last letters of each word taken in turn then spell out the word alphabetical.

   AppraisaL, PublisH, AbsorB, ExpliciT, IroniC, ArboreaL

2 Imagine that her twin leaves the hotel at the top of the mountain at exactly the same time as she leaves from the bottom of the mountain, i.e. 6 a.m. Then further imagine that they both reach their destination at the same time, 6 p.m. They must, therefore, pass each other on the trail as they both make exactly the same journey. It is at this specific time that they are at the same spot at exactly the

same time. While the puzzle does not give sufficient
information to determine at which point they pass each
other, it does enable us to prove that such a point and
time must exist.

3   The missing shape is a square. Looking across each line,
the number of sides in the shape in the final figure is the
sum of the number of sides in the first two figures.
Looking down the number of sides in the final figure is
the difference in the number of sides in the first two
figures.

4   82246; in all the other numbers the first two digits
multiplied by 4 equal the last three digits, for example
$45 \times 4 = 180$. With 82246, $82 \times 3 = 246$.

5   Like so many puzzles, this looks far more complicated
than it really is. In fact, it has a beautifully simple
solution. The trick is first of all to work out how long it
takes the man to walk home. You know that the dog has
been running for all of this time at a constant speed, so it
is then a simple matter to work out how many miles it
has covered in this period.
   In this case, the man walks for 7 miles at 3 m.p.h.,
which means he takes 2.33 hours or 2 hours 20 minutes.
The dog is, therefore, running for 2.33 hours at 8 m.p.h,
which means it covers $18^2/_3$ miles.

6   C; all the others are symmetric about a horizontal axis,
i.e. they appear the same turned upside down.

7   GRAMMAR; each word starts with the letter whose
position in the alphabet coincides with the number of
letters in the preceding word. JUBILEE has seven letters,

so the next word GRAMMAR, starts with the seventh
letter of the alphabet.

8   4; convert the numbers into Roman numerals – viii, ii, iv,
x, vi, i, iii, iv.

9   6; read down the first column of letters and back up the
second etc. to spell out the message 'decipher this
message to choose number six'.

10   5050; if the numbers 1–100 are written out 1, 2, 3, 4 ...
97, 98, 99, 100, it can be seen that each opposite pair of
numbers totals 101 (i.e. 100 + 1, 99 + 2, 98 + 3 etc.,
down to 50 + 51). As there are 100 numbers there must
be 50 such pairs. The sum, therefore, is 101 × 50 = 5050.

11

14	1	7	4
3	12	9	16
10	15	5	13
6	8	11	2

So that:
(i)   no consecutive numbers appear in any horizontal,
vertical or diagonal line from which it follows that:
(ii)   no two consecutive numbers appear adjacent
(horizontally, vertically or diagonally).

12   49 times in 50, or 98%.
Again, let's set up a tree diagram. Assume that Calamity
Jane goes first:

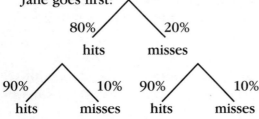

Look to see which branches lead to the target being hit.

If it is hit and then hit again, that counts; if it is hit and then missed, that counts; if it is missed and then hit, that counts; if both miss it, that does not count. Therefore, multiply along the first three branches and add:

$(.8 \times .9) + (.8 \times .1) + (.2 \times .9) =$
$.72 + .08 + .18 = .98$, or 98%.

13 They all have aquatic creatures hidden within them:
   Duk(e El)lington
   The (New T)estament
   A red (carp)et
   The game of S(crab)ble
   The Morse (Cod)e

14 They never will. In a five-segment figure, two places anticlockwise is the same as three moves clockwise. The two objects will simply change places at each stage.

15 197; reading back to front reveals the sequence of odd numbers, 1, 3, 5, 7, 9, 11, 13, 15, 17, 19, 31, 23, 25 in groups of three digits.

16 4.8 m.p.h.; say that his journey was 6 miles each way. Then, at 6 m.p.h. the outward jog would take 1 hour and the inward walk 1.5 hours. This means that it takes 2.5 hours to travel 12 miles, or 1 hour to travel 4.8 miles.

17 87: arrange the digits 783 in every possible way and divide by 9.
   $378/9 = 42$
   $387/9 = 43$
   $783/9 = \mathbf{87}$

738/9 = 82
837/9 = 93
873/9 = 97

18 Phil painted six more than Ken irrespective of how many
   lampposts there were in the street.
   If P is the number of lampposts:
   Phil painted P – 3 + 6 = P + 3
   Ken painted 3 + P – 6 = P – 3
   So Phil painted 6 more than Ken, whatever the value of P.

19 (b) eat humble pie; each phrase begins with the middle
       two letters of the previous phrase.

20 E; the others spell words – elf, cell, fee, clef, fell – when
   read vertically with their mirror image. In other words,
   cover the left-hand half of each set of figures to read the
   words downwards.

21 0; somewhere in the calculation is x – x, which is zero.
   Any series of numbers multiplied together gives the
   answer 0 if zero is one of the numbers in the series.

22 N   N   O   U
   Start at the top and alternate from column to column to
   spell out four words:
   MAGNIFICATION – columns 1 and 3
   SUPERSTITIOUS – columns 2 and 4
   ADVERTISEMENT – columns 3 and 1
   INSIGNIFICANT – columns 4 and 2

23 BATON; in all the others one of the 5-letter words is an
   anagram of the last 5 letters of one of the 10-letter
   words:

PARAGLIDER – RILED, SUMMERTIME – MERIT,
CONTINUITY – UNITY, BALUSTRADE – RATED,
PRIMORDIAL – LAIRD, EMBITTERED – DETER,
LAMENTABLE – BLEAT

24 SOFTWARE; it's an anagram of far + twoEs

25 A name is spelled out by the second, fourth and sixth
    letters of each word – Don, Ted, Una, Ned, Ray and Sue.

26 The chances of a black pair were zero as there were
    three white socks and one black sock in the drawer.

    The chances are as follows: W1, W2, W3, B1

White pair	Mixed pair	Black pair	
W1–W2	W1–B1		
W1–W3	W2–B1		
W2–W3	W3–B1		
3	3	0	
Chances =			
½	½	0	= 1

If there had been two white socks and two black socks in the
drawer, the chances of a white pair would be ¼, not ½.

White pair	Mixed pair	Black pair	
W1–W2	W1–B1	B1–B2	
	W1–B2		
W2–W1	W2–B1		
	W2–B2	B2–B1	
2	4	2	
Chances =			
¼	½	¼	= 1

27 Hole 6

Hole	A Even	B Odd	C Prime	D Square	E Cube	F One
1		✓		✓	✓	✓
2	✓		✓			
3		✓	✓			
4	✓			✓		
5		✓	✓			
6	✓					
7		✓	✓			
8	✓				✓	
9		✓		✓		
10	✓					✓
11		✓	✓			✓
12	✓					✓
13		✓	✓			✓
14	✓					✓
15		✓				✓
16	✓			✓		✓
17		✓	✓			✓
18	✓					✓

Hole 6 is the only one with one tick.

28 There were 37 flutes in the consignment.

The 1st took $^{37}/_{19} = 1^{18}/_{19} + ^1/_{19} = 2$

The 2nd took $^{35}/_{18} = 1^{17}/_{18} + ^1/_{18} = 2$

and so on.

The 2nd from last took $^3/_2 + ^1/_2 = 2$

There were 37 flutes in the consignment so 18 had 2 each and the last one had the only one left.

29 1¼ hours

    Reciprocal 6 = ⅙ = .166
    Reciprocal 3 = ⅓ = .333
    Reciprocal 5 = ⅕ = .2
    Reciprocal 10 = ¹⁄₁₀ = .1
                        .8   Add

    Now take reciprocal again $\dfrac{1}{.8}$ = 1.25 hours

30 CHINCHILLA

31 Yes. Alan accepted Bill's bet and handed over £2. Bill
    reneged on the bet and handed over £1, making a profit
    of £1.

32 No, it is not a fair bet because a punter on a winning
    streak can only win $1000:

Bank	$1000
Win	500
Win	250
Win	125
Win	62.50

and so on. The punter can only win $1000.

A punter on a losing streak can lose a fortune:

Bank	$1000
Lose	500
Lose	750
Lose	1125
Lose	1687.50
Lose	2531.25

33 8, 5; the numbers represent the number of letters in each word in the question.

34 10080; $2 \times 7!$ or $2 \times 7 \times 6 \times 5 \times 4 \times 3 \times 2 \times 1$

35 Imagine a fifth of the column wrapped in paper. When unravelled it will equal a size of $40' \times 16'\ 8''$ with the garland shown as a diagonal line across corner to corner. Therefore the garland would equal $43'\ 4'' \times 5 = 216'\ 8''$.

36 It contains the numbers 1–9 in alphabetical order.

37 15,599 to 1

$$1\text{st} = \frac{1}{26}$$

$$2\text{nd} = \frac{1}{25}$$

$$3\text{rd} = \frac{1}{24}$$

$$26 \times 25 \times 24 = 15,600$$

38 6210001000

39 $869 + 702 + 413 = 1984$; 5 omitted.

40
	H		E		L	
ZABXG		ILCMD		FAYOK		MCBEO
	P		M		E	
	QSIUL		NCAPD		FGIAE	

41 One; from the box marked WB draw a marble; if it is white, the other marble must be white (WW). The box labelled WW must be BB and the box labelled BB must be WB.

42 190; 19 + 18 + 17 + 16 + 15 + 14 + 13 + 12 + 11 +
    10 + 9 + 8 + 7 + 6 + 5 + 4 + 3 + 2 + 1

43 1st   27
    2nd 25
    3rd 18
    4th 16
    5th 14

44 The fish weighed 144 oz.

Head	54 oz
Body	72 oz
Tail	18 oz

45 234 – 144 = 90
    213 – 144 = 69
    90 + 69 + 144 = 303 people surveyed, not 300.

46 YOGA; each word starts with the letter that completed
    the previous word.

47 Tom   7 years
    Molly   13 years

48 They all carry an animal in reverse.

    rEPAst
    hUNGry
    dEODar
    sTACked
    sTARlight
    miSSAl

49 1 °C, –1 °C, 2 °C, –2 °C, 3 °C,

    $1 \times 2 \times 3 = 6 \times -1 = -6 \times -1 = +12$

50 10

$85 + 75 + 60 + 90 = 310$ objects

$310 = 100 \times 3$ with 10 left over

Agility of mind

1 (i)   M   (vi)   R
  (ii) Q   (vii) Z
  (iii) C   (viii) N
  (iv) O   (ix)   U
  (v)   L   (x)   D

Rating:
10   very impressive
9   exceptional
7–8 excellent
5–6 good
3–4 average
0–2 you panicked!

2 (a) 13   (i) 6734
  (b) 138269   (j) 39
  (c) 9   (k) 26583
  (d) 5789   (l) 47591
  (e) 5748361   (m) 495
  (f) 2136   (n) 48519
  (g) 73964   (o) 459
  (h) 5694

Rating:

15	very impressive
13–14	exceptional
11–12	excellent
8–10	very good
6–7	good
5	average

3 Answers:
   (i)   C; all the others have an identical pairing.
   (ii) C; all the others have all their sides equal.
   (iii) C; in all the others one dot is in one circle and the other dot is in two circles.
   (iv) E; all the others have a mirror-image pairing.
   (v)   D; it spirals clockwise, all the others spiral anticlockwise.
   (vi) B; its curved side is concave, in all the others the curved side is convex.
   (vii) A; all the others are four-sided figures.
   (viii) C; the rest are the same figure rotated.
   (ix) B; the rest are divided into four identical segments.
   (x)   B; the only one in which the dot appears in more than one figure.

Rating:

10	very impressive
9	exceptional
7–8	excellent
6	very good
5	good
4	average

4 (i)   48931   (ix) 2468931
   (ii) 28975   (x)   2469731
   (iii) 24691   (xi) 2468973
   (iv) 246873   (xii) 2897531
   (v)   497531   (xiii) 2468971
   (vi) 246951   (xiv) 24689753
   (vii) 2897531   (xv) 26897531
   (viii) 2469531

Rating:
15   very impressive
13–14   exceptional
11–12   excellent
8–10   very good
6–7   good
5   average

5

L	A	G	O	O	N		A		M	A	D	E
	L		W		E	D	I	F	Y		A	
S	P	O	N	G	E		S		N	O	N	E
	H		E		D	E	L	T	A		C	
F	A	I	R	L	Y		E		H	E	E	L
E		N		A		K		B	R		R	O
N	E	T		I	D	E	A	L		A	R	C
C		E		R		Y		U		S		A
E	A	R	N		T		R	E	V	E	A	L
	L		A	W	A	S	H		A		B	
S	E	N	D		C		Y	E	L	L	O	W
	R		I	D	I	O	M		U		V	
S	T	A	R		T		E	L	E	V	E	N

6 (i) A and E
   (ii) 36 litres
   (iii) 72
   (iv) ¾ or 0.75
   (v) D
   (vi) 16
   (vii) A and C
   (viii) 14 : 21 (15 : 21 appears exactly the same in its mirror image)
   (ix) 15 minutes
   (x) 4; there are two alternate sequences, 1, 2, 3, 4 and 3, 4, 5.

Rating:
10   very impressive
9   exceptional
7–8 excellent
6   very good
5   good
4   average

7 (i) $9 + 64 = 73$ (vi) $64 + 17 = 81$
   (ii) $88 + 27 = 115$ (vii) $9 + 27 = 36$
   (iii) $17 + 95 = 112$ (viii) $9 + 88 = 97$
   (iv) $9 + 6 = 15$ (ix) $83 + 64 = 147$
   (v) $88 + 83 = 171$ (x) $95 + 64 = 159$

8 (i) $4 + 2 = 6$ (vi) $4 \div 2 = 2$
   (ii) $4 - 2 = 2$ (vii) $2 \times 2 = 4$
   (iii) $0 + 2 = 2$ (viii) $3 \div 3 = 1$
   (iv) $2 \times 2 = 4$ (ix) $2 \times 0 = 0$
   (v) $4 - 1 = 3$ (x) $3 - 2 = 1$

9 (i) 5   (vi) 1
  (ii) 20   (vii) 12
 (iii) 13   (viii) 2
 (iv) 4   (ix) 1
  (v) 4   (x) 4

10 (i) 2E, 5B, 7G   (vi) 3C, 6F
   (ii) 2D, 4B   (vii) 2C, 3B, 4E, 5D
  (iii) 3F, 5G, 6C, 7E   (viii) 1A, 1D, 4A
  (iv) 2G, 3D, 4C, 7B   (ix) 4F, 6D
   (v) 1C, 1G, 2B, 2F, 3A, 3G   (x) 5F, 6E
       4D, 6B, 6G, 7A, 7C, 7F

IQ test one

Spatial ability test

1 D; A and E are identical with black/white reversal, as are C and B.

2 E; the sequence runs triangle/semicircle/circle, and horizontal stripe/black/vertical stripe/checked.

3 D; the semicircle rotates 180° and goes in the square, the rectangle rotates 90° and attaches itself to the bottom of the square.

4 E; in each row and column, only when a circle appears in the same position in the first two squares is it transferred to the final square, but then changes black to white and vice versa.

5 C; at each alternate stage the top part moves down, similarly at the other alternate stage the bottom line moves up.

6 A

7 B; at alternate stages the figure on the right moves left, and the figure on the left moves right. The figure in the middle retains its position.

8 D; the rest are the same figure rotated.

9 B; at each stage the largest arc moves 90° anticlockwise. The other two arcs move 90° clockwise at each stage.

10 D; a white dot is transferred to the final pentagon when it appears in the same position once in the previous three pentagons. A black dot is transferred when it appears twice.

Logical test

1 N   B
   A   G

G	B	F	G	A	F	N	A	C	N
F	K	A	B	N	G	C	F	K	A
A	C	N	K	C	B	K	G	B	F
N	N	C	C	K	K	B	B	G	G
C	A	K	N	B	C	G	K	F	B
K	F	B	A	G	N	F	C	A	K
B	G	G	F	F	A	A	N	N	C
G	B	F	G	A	F	N	A	C	N
F	K	A	B	N	G	C	F	K	A
A	C	N	K	C	B	K	G	B	F

The letters AFGBKCN are being repeated following the path shown above.

2 d) 364478

ABCDEF   DFBECA

847346   364478

3 Tom

4 8
    6

4	3	8	7	5	6
2	5	7	6	8	5
7	8	1	8	7	6
5	4	7	6	4	8
3	8	6	3	8	7
7	2	5	8	6	4

The grid contains 1×1, 2×2, 3×3, 4×4, 5×5, 6×6, 7×7 and 8×8.
All numbers are then placed in the grid so that the same number is never horizontally or vertically adjacent.

5 WINDSWEPT; the letters SET are moving up one place each time:
    ScEpTical
    aSpEcTual
    inSpEcTor
    proSpEcTs
    windSwEpT

6

At each stage the little hand moves two back and the big hand moves two forward.

7 UC; U is the 21st letter of the alphabet from the beginning and C is the 24th from the end.

8 CEJH; starting at the first letter, jump to alternate letters of the alphabet to obtain the next three letters but change round the order of the last two letters. The set CEJH jumps three letters from E to H. The correct sequence would be CEIG.

9 198; reverse 81 and put these numbers first and last. The middle number is 8 + 1.

10 Two chances in three. Call the balls, either of which may be put in the empty bag first, B1 and W, and call the black ball, which you see go in, B2. After the black ball has been taken out there are three possibilities.

    1) B1 still in the bag, B2 outside
    2) B2 still in the bag, B1 outside
    3) W still in the bag, B2 outside

Of these options, there is only one in which the white ball is still in the bag.

Verbal test

1 ant; to give pant, meant, scant, want, rant.

2 MONTAGE; the rest are figures of speech.

3 decrease, boost

4 monastic, austere

5 amethyst; to give pea, rim, pie, met, ash, buy, has, sat.

6 b) WATT : POWER

7 reinvent the wheel

8 eyed guide

9 blood-curdling

10 threat

Numbers

1 2; $12 + 4 = 16$, $5 + 3 = 8$, $16 \div 8 = 2$

2 2; look across at numbers in the same position in each pentagon.

$6 + 1 + 3 = 10$, $2 + 4 + 4 = 10$

3 5963: $16 + 43 = 59$, $31 + 31 = 62$

4 92.5; the amount deducted each time increases by 0.5.

5 2 minutes 15 seconds

$$(1.25 + 0.25) \times \frac{60}{40}$$

$$1.5 \times \frac{60}{40} = \frac{90}{40} = 2.25 \text{ or 2 minutes 15 seconds}$$

6 17; start at 2 and jump to alternate segments adding 1, 2, 3, 4, 5, 6.

7 7; $\dfrac{15 + 17 - 11}{3} = 7$

8 4; $2 \times 9 = 18$, $9 \times 8 = 72$, $72/18 = 4$.

9 122; the difference is multiplied by 3 each time, i.e. 1, 3, 9, 27, 81.

10 29; $4 \times 9 = 36 - 7 = 29$

IQ test two

Spatial ability test

1 B

2 D; A is the same as G, B is the same as E, C is the same as F.

3 2A

4 E; R is added to S to make T, 1 is added to 2 to make 3. Like symbols disappear.

5 C

6 3; B is added to A = C, C is added to D = E,
    E is added to F = G, G is added to H = A.
    Like symbols disappear.

7 E; number of lines in X = 8. A = 5, B = 6, C = 7, D = 6,
    E = 8.

8 B; 1 + 2 = 3, 4 + 5 = 6, 7 + 8 = 9, 6 + 9 = 10.
    Like symbols disappear.

9 A

10 E

Logic test
  1 27.3 km

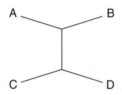

  2 If using both sides of the scale: 1
                                            3
                                            9
                                           27

      If using only one pan: 1
                                            2
                                            4
                                            8
                                           16
                                           32

3 26 to 10

	Die 1					
	1	2	3	4	5	6
Die 2 1	1	1	1	1	1	1
2	2	2	2	2	2	2
3	3	3	3	3	3	3
4	4	4	4	4	4	4
5	5	5	5	5	5	5
6	6	6	6	6	6	6

4 The same; if one pair has all of the diamonds the other pair has none.

5 He was born on 29th February 1896. There wasn't a leap year in 1900 so the next one will be 29th February 1904.

6 E; number of angles is increasing by 1 each time.

7 3.3; take all of the differences between 0 and 9, add them together and divide by the number of differences

$$= \frac{333}{100} = 3.3$$

8 The total will oscillate between 0 and 9.

9 7! (7 factional) or $7 \times 6 \times 5 \times 4 \times 3 \times 2 \times 1 = 5040$.

10 24; opposite sides of a die total 7, so the number 3 is on the face opposite the number 4.

Verbal ability test
1 INVEIGLE, PERSUADE

2 c) STALK

3 d) A DITCH

4 LARK

5 b) MARCASITE

6 PERIPHERAL

7 HOMAGE

8 a) FUNAMBULIST

9 INFIRMITY, STRENGTH

10 WAPNOT (BANANA, LICHEE, ORANGE, NUTMEG)

Numerical ability test
1 14

$$18 + 18 = 36 \qquad 6 + 14 = 20 \qquad 36 + 26 = 62$$
$$17 + 19 = 36 \qquad 11 + 9 = 20 \qquad 40 + 22 = 62$$
$$6 + 30 = 36 \qquad 19 + 1 = 20 \qquad 48 + 14 = 62$$

2 38½

Jump two segments: 7, 11½, 16, 20½, 25, 29½, 34, 38½ (+4½)

3 12

$$12 \div 4 = 3 \qquad 15 \div 5 = 3 \qquad 14 \div 7 = 2$$

$$44 \div 11 = 4 \qquad 120 \div 60 = 2 \qquad 90 \div 15 = 6$$
$$3 \times 4 = 12 \qquad 3 \times 2 = 6 \qquad 2 \times 6 = 12$$

4 50; (first column × 3rd column) – second column.

5 0.10; there are two series, –0.19 and +0.19

0.67, 0.48, 0.29, 0.10
0.69, 0.88, 1.07, 1.26

6 –46

$16 - (63) + 4 - (3) = 16 - 63 + 4 - 3 = 46$
(×, ÷) must be evaluated before (+, –).

7 ½

$$\frac{6}{17} \div \frac{24}{34} = \frac{6}{17} \times \frac{34}{24} = \frac{2}{4} = \frac{1}{2}$$

8 $20\frac{1}{36}$

$$2\frac{1}{4} + 17\frac{7}{9} = 2\frac{9}{36} + 17\frac{28}{36} = 19\frac{37}{36} = 20\frac{1}{36}$$

9 8; opposite outer numbers and inner numbers add up to the same.

10 84; (6 + 2 + 7) × 4 (8 + 3 + 3) × 2
(16 + 1 + 11) × 3